The Grandparents' Book

The Grandparents' Book

By Anastazia and Stuart Little

Illustrations by Roy McKie

Design • Anthony LaSala
Production • Akiko Taniyama

Published by Spectacle Lane Press

All rights reserved
Text Copyright © 1988 by Anastazia and Stuart Little
Illustrations © 1988 by Roy McKie

This book may not be reproduced in whole or in part,
by any means, without permission.
For information address:

Spectacle Lane Press, Box 34, Georgetown, CT 06829

ISBN 0-930753-04-6

Published simultaneously in the United States and Canada
Printed in the United States of America

Photos of authors and grandchildren by Christopher Little.

Page 35, Excerpt from "Dunbarton" from LIFE STUDIES by Robert Lowell, Copyright © 1956, 1959 by Robert Lowell. Reprinted by permission of Farrar, Straus and Giroux, Inc.

Page 58, Excerpt from MY NAME IS ARAM, copyright 1938, 1966 by William Saroyan. Reprinted by permission of Harcourt Brace Jovanovich, Inc.

Page 91, Excerpt from "Generations of Men" from NORTH OF BOSTON by Robert Frost. Copyright by Robert Frost. Reprinted by permission of Holt, Rinehart & Winston, Inc.

Page 92, Excerpt from THE GRAPES OF WRATH by John Steinbeck. Copyright 1939 by John Steinbeck, renewed © 1967 by John Steinbeck. All rights reserved. Reprinted by permission of Viking Penguin, Inc.

About the Authors:

Both the authors of *The Grandparents' Book,* Anastazia and Stuart Little and illustrator Roy McKie are three-time grandparents. But, typical of the modern breed, they haven't been slowed up much by grandparenthood.

Long-time New York City residents, the Littles busily pursue literary activities (he's a writer and editor; she's a playwright) in their SoHo apartment. Weekends, they are off to their summer home in Connecticut, where she cooks and gardens. He pulls his quota of weeds before heading

 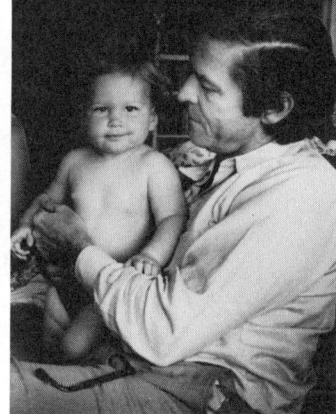 

Anastazia and Jonathan **Melissa and Stuart** **Artist Roy McKie**

for the tennis court or golf course, where he struggles to hold down a handicap which, he says, "has grown right along with my grandchildren."

One of the most prolific and published cartoonists, Roy McKie has contributed to hundreds of books and done thousands of illustrations for magazines and other media over a 40-year career that is still going strong. Habitually a man on the move, McKie gets his exercise by biking and walking. He is also an inveterate traveler, who, as he does in his drawings, is constantly seeking the new and different path.

CONTENTS

About the Authors 5

CHAPTERS:

1. Birth to Two: FIRST ENCOUNTERS 9

2. Three to Five: SMALL CHALLENGES 23

3. Six to Eight: AHEAD OF THE (CON) GAME ...43

4. Nine to Twelve: CHANGE THE SUBJECT BEFORE YOU LOSE THE ARGUMENT 57

5. Thirteen to Seventeen: WHEN SMILES TURN TO SCOWLS ...71

6. Eighteen Up: ADDING UP THE SCORE 85

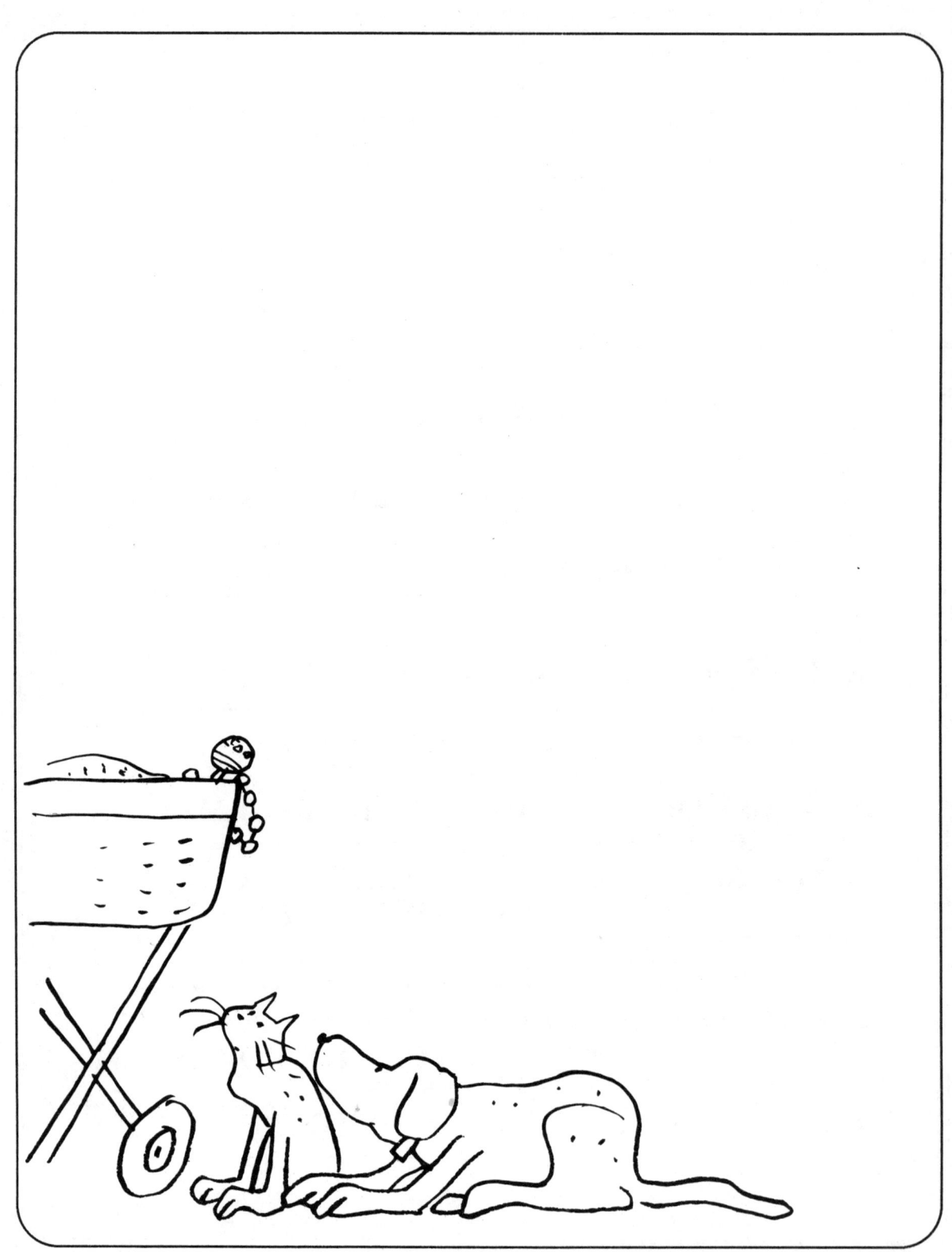

1. Birth to Two:

FIRST ENCOUNTERS

In the beginning, the grandchild responds to your attention only with cries of rage or hunger. Nevertheless, you keep up a stream of cheerful chatter as you hug and feed. One day, you will suddenly be rewarded by... a smile!
And then, just as suddenly, this passive bundle turns into a wriggler and takes off. Manipulating, asserting, experimenting, testing your patience. Wonderful.

There they were, a middle-aged couple, suddenly free of parental responsibility. Their youngest child had just graduated from college and for the first time in over twenty years there was some excess cash floating around and, of course, time.

The husband thought he could manage the family business from home now, and he might even go to art school a couple of evenings a week. The wife contemplated cutting down on her manuscript reading and maybe taking a course in Chinese cooking. And they could both go to tennis camp this summer. Yes, now they were free to plan their activities without regard to anyone's needs or schedules except their own. And then, suddenly, their eldest daughter called to say she was pregnant.

"Pregnant! Did you hear that? We'll be grandparents!"

The father cast a sidelong glance in the mirror.

"I'm too young to be a grandfather," he said. "I'm only forty-eight."

"Don't be silly. Think of the 'continuity of life,' our life."

"We won't be expected to babysit?"

"Oh, once in a while, maybe. No, babysitting's not our concern. We simply won't always be available."

"I'd hate to give up our plans."

"No need. We're only the grandparents."

The future grandfather mulled things over for a minute or two. Then he announced:

"Let's keep this under our hats for a while, until I get used to the idea. I must find a way of showing my friends that I haven't become Old Father Time overnight."

When the news did slip out he was relieved to see how solicitous and understated the comments of his friends were.

One simply said, "Good luck."

"I'll drink to that," said another.

They studiously avoided any reference to his age, which did help him to prepare for his new role. And sometimes he'd find himself walking past a school and actually noticing the younger children. By the time the baby arrived, and he had held it in his arms, he was well on his way to being hooked. The grandmother had been hooked from the start.

Along with the pleasures of the new state came certain apprehensions. For instance, did they remember the old rules? Be firm and convincing. Start off the way you mean to continue, they told themselves. Forgotten skills came to mind. Carrying techniques: When the baby can sit up, place it on your hip, to divide the weight. For the future, diversionary tactics: Change the subject before you lose the argument.

"Right, and never let yourself be boxed in," said the grandfather.

They laughed at how little they had forgotten. But in fact, there was no real need for them to bother to remember. The parents preferred to manage on their own, naturally enough. But the grandparents secretly thought the children were silly not to take advantage of so much well-seasoned advice. It was free, it could cut corners. At the outset, they gave a suggestion or two to their daughter, such as: "Why don't you tilt the bottle, dear, so the baby doesn't swallow a whole lot of air? Because we all know that air leads to gas, and gas is followed by crying, and crying causes sleepless nights."

But the daughter's reaction to this gentle suggestion was quite extreme: "All right, all right, we know you know that, Mother, but we want to find these things out for ourselves, because, you see, this is our child."

Which should prompt you never to start a sentence with: "If it were *my* child..."

Learning this preliminary lesson, the grandparents were as far as possible spectators. "Don't say a word," they told each other, when the baby cried and was not picked up quickly enough, or was picked up too quickly. When there was no firm hand under its wobbling head, or when there was a pacifier in its mouth even while it slept. Yet privately they reserved for themselves the right to interject their own philosophy when the grandchild was older and they were alone with it.

So during that first year the grandparents did have time for their new interests. They saw their grandchild often and watched him develop, though always in

"Don't say a word!"

the company of his parents. Between themselves they shared little jokes, calling him the "tiger in the playpen" and, because of the results of his insatiable appetite, "Old Thunderthighs."

When remonstrating was in order, the parents said, "You go home, we'll handle it." And so they coasted along with this delightfully non-obtrusive baby until, suddenly, the routine changed.

One evening they said, "We're off now, we're catching a movie at eight."

"Oh, can't you stay until the next show?" the daughter begged. "We've been asked out for drinks and this would give you a nice chance to get to know your grandson." They looked at each other.

"Don't worry," the son-in-law added. "We'll pick him up at your house."

"He's a good boy, sleeps through the whole night now, don't you, monkey?" The mother gave him a smacking kiss. "Oh, and if he cries just give him his bottle. We won't be late."

"Well, there goes the movie," the grandfather said when they were gone.

"But I could hardly refuse the very first time we were asked to help. Why don't you go, there's no need for us both to stay home."

"I want us to see it together."

And that was just the beginning of their grandparental tour of duty. The parents returned at 1:24 a.m.

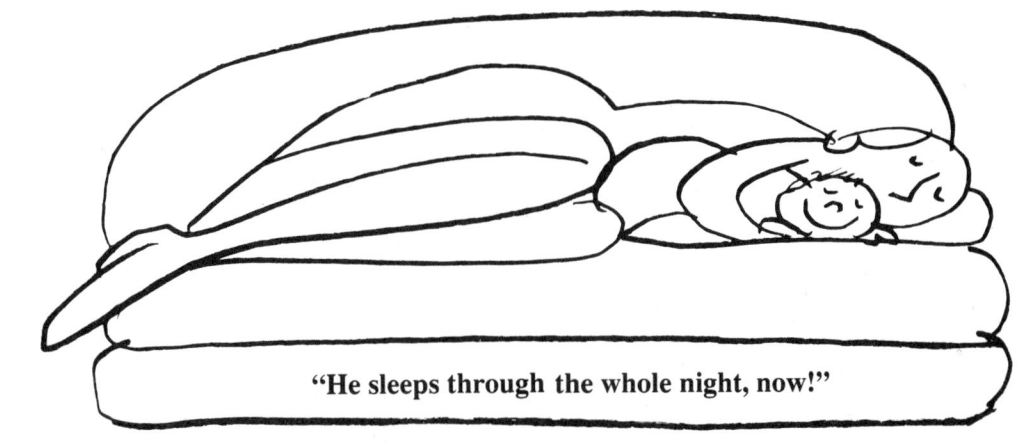

"He sleeps through the whole night, now!"

"It's the big brown eyes!"

Between the grandparents, initially, there was a certain amount of chill as to whether the child took after his or her family.

"I'll grant you the mouth and even the chin," she said, "but if ever I saw an exact copy of my mother's nose, there it is on that baby's face."

"Oh, to hell with the nose," he said irritably. "It's the big brown eyes. There's no mistaking that those eyes come from my side. Eyes, the most important feature, the 'mirror of the soul,'" he added.

Rather pompously, she thought.

• • • • •

The grandparents arrived in Florida. This would be the first time they had seen their granddaughter. An exciting day. The weather was glorious as they got off the plane, although the grandmother could still feel the effects of a chilled-to-the-bone Maine winter. Consequently, when their daughter asked on the next morning if they'd "mind the baby for an hour or so and please take her outside," the grandmother agonized. How should she dress her? What should she wear? Eventually, on a high shelf in a suitcase she found a sleeping pouch with hood attached. Finally she swaddled the child in a blanket, and proudly went out to show her grandchild to the world. The grandfather followed, reluctantly, but he needed his exercise.

The baby cried. How to get her to sleep? The grandmother turned the carriage backwards to avoid eye contact. The cries grew more desperate and spots appeared on her red face.

"Could she have developed measles the first time we took her out?" Grandmother asked her husband when he hurried up.

"Prickly heat," he said, puffing.
"In Maine? Unheard of!"
"We're in Florida now, dear."

• • • • •

There were certain changes, however, that the grandmother needed to understand. New contrivances and gadgets. The grandfather didn't concern himself much with these. He clung to the old traditions —caring for the baby was women's work. "I'm not being chauvinistic. I'm a pre-role-reversal man, that's all," he said, picking up the baby and bouncing it on his knee. The grandmother wondered how long this resolve would last.

So the grandmother set about learning the new ways. Learning to put diapers on with Velcro fastenings instead of safety pins and avoiding the pricking and fumbling. And why had nobody thought up paper diapers twenty odd years ago? And the food. Everything thrown into the blender, cheeses and spices and calves' liver.

The playpen was obsolete, replaced by a movable bouncing seat. A plastic window prevented rain from falling into the baby carriage. All of which was sensible. However, the grandmother felt she should comment at the sight of her grandchild seated in a sort of bo's'n's chair, his face inches from the mother's chest. "It would be nice if he had a broader panorama," she ventured. "We don't want a crisis when he realizes there's more to the world than the front of a sweater."

• • • • •

While bribery should not be a general rule, grandparents are human. If you want your grandchild to come straight to you in a roomful of people competing for the attention of the entering baby, simply put a favorite toy on your lap. When he reaches for it, scoop him up, press him tightly against you, and enjoy the admiration of the assembled company.

• • • • •

Stifle those stabs of jealousy when the treasured grandchild abandons you for a visitor performing magic tricks. Be philosophical. Recognize that this is a good way to improve the child's concentration and buy a magic trick book yourself.

The "other" grandparents.

Before the other grandparents arrive, you decide it would be unbecoming to compete with them. So stand back. Let them feed, dress, read to, and cuddle the grandchild, knowing that you could do equally well and can resume your rightful place as soon as they've gone.

• • • • •

Grandfather has been pressed into shelling peas and the little one is anxious to help.

"No, sorry, wait till you're bigger," Grandfather says.

The grandchild starts to whine.

"Dinner's behind schedule as it is," fusses the grandmother.

But the grandfather, realizing this was

(continued on next page)

no answer for a three-year-old, produces a flashlight, turns it on, and the child is enchanted when the beam catches his face. "All right," says Grandfather. "Use that flashlight, soon as a pea falls, down on your knees, under that table, find that pea!"

Sometimes the grandchild forgets and holds the beam up toward the ceiling, thereby crushing a few peas on the floor with his knees. So what? He's now part of the action and he's stopped whining.

• • • • •

Here are the grandparents, puttering around the garden. He mows the lawn with gusto, she transplants seedlings in a more dignified manner. The little girl totters and stumbles down the pebble path, which was laid by the elder generation.

"Careful," they tell her automatically. "No stumbling!" They are always nervous when left in charge. The responsibility...

She smiles, happy to be free of a restraining hand. Inevitably, she falls. Granny throws down her trowel. Grandpa leaves the lawn mower, motor running. Together, they pick her up as she roars her outrage. He produces a large handkerchief to dry the tears.

She hides her face.

Granny gets down on her hands and knees. "Are you all right, love? Are you all right?"

"Here." A knee is raised for inspection.

"No broken bones, no broken skin, just a small discoloration," Grandpa announces.

"No need for the emergency room. Just hurt feelings."

"Thank God," they whisper in chorus.

"This calls for a Bandaid," says Granny.

The victim attempts a smile. "Please, and one for my mosquito bite."

In fact, recovery is often hastened if this formula is followed: One Bandaid for a bruise, two for a bump, and so on...

• • • • •

No need for the emergency room. Just hurt feelings.

Questionnaire for Grandfathers

(To rate yourself as a grandfather, give one answer in each category and consult the numerical equivalent of each answer on the following page.)

1. Did you object to becoming a grandfather? (a) Yes____ (b) No____
   If yes, why? (c) Too young____ (d) Too busy____ (e) Too sporty____ (f) Didn't care____
2. What did you feel when you first saw the grandchild? (a) Love____
   (b) Pride____ (c) Amazement____ (d) Terror____ (e) Gloom____ (f) Rage____
3. Did you resist becoming a grandfather by
   (a) Pretending you didn't belong to the crying baby?____
   (b) Not taking your turn pushing the carriage?____
   (c) Removing yourself from the whole experience by hiding behind the newspaper?____

   or
4. Did you fall in line by
   (a) Bragging about the child?____
   (b) Carrying photographs?____
   (c) Testing the patience of your friends?____

   or
   Did you revolt? If so, there is no need to continue this questionnaire.
5. Presuming you overcame any initial distaste for the grandchild, at what point did this conversion occur?
   (a) After an hour?____ (b) When he started showing you affection?____ (c) When he developed a sense of humor?____
6. How often do you see your grandchild?
   (a) Once a week?____ (b) Once a month?____ (c) Once a year?____
7. (a) Do you telephone often?____ (b) Send cards?____ (c) Send funny cards?____
8. Has your life gone back to normal? (a) Yes____ (b) No____ (c) Nearly____

Quiz Answers and Points

1. a=0; b=8; c=6; d=4; e=4; f=1.
2. a=8; b=4; c=6; d=2; e=0; f=0.
3. a=1; b=2; c=6.
4. a=4; b=6; c=8.
5. a=4; b=2; c=8.
6. a=8; b=6; c=2.
7. a=6; b=6; c=8.
8. a=8; b=4; c=2.

Now, add up your points and rate yourself as a grandfather:

If you scored 55 or better	You are nominated Grandfather of the Year.
45-54	Basically, you did want to be a grandfather, you just had to try it first.
35-44	A certain hesitancy here, but the signs indicate a willingness to improve.
25-34	Work on it, keep it up. Could be you should involve yourself more in the child's activities.
0-24	Seems like you are a hopeless case.

In answer to this questionnaire, Bob Hope said:
(a) He did not object to becoming a grandfather.
(b) He did feel he was too young.
(c) His first reactions on meeting the newborn grandchild were (1) pleasure and (2) "other."

• • • • •

It is frustrating for a child who has finally learned to talk to discover he is not always understood. No wonder he kicks up a fuss when his grandfather offers to take him for a walk. "What?" says the grandfather, often making the child repeat himself. It is equally frustrating for the older person, though he should remind himself that newly learned words tend to be whispered. A compromise might be reached if, on the walk, routes were picked for their low walls and other raised surfaces to allow the two to be nearer each other's level.

You can't take your eyes off the grandchild for a minute. If you should, don't be surprised to look up and find him scampering around the kitchen brandishing a carving knife. Strategy is called for here. It's the shininess that attracts him. Wad up a sheet of silver foil into a ball. As he reaches, hold out your decoy and remove the knife without comment.

• • • • •

What grandmother could resist producing a popsicle after "I love you" has been whispered in her ear, even though she knows the little one's attention is focussed on the open freezer door.

• • • • •

When all your shoes are thrown down the stairs by an imp, instead of engaging in a tussle, which you find you often lose, try a silent tack. There is no fun in naughtiness if the adult doesn't rise to the bait, so when no words are exchanged, the game is soon over. Of course, this usually means you must pick up the shoes yourself, but that's a small price to pay for avoiding future tussles.

• • • • •

When you ask your little granddaughter to kiss an old aunt who is making a rare visit, and the baby shies away from the unfamiliar face, you find yourself in a dilemma. Should you insist on obedience, or risk seeming weak in the eyes of your aunt? Actually, neither alternative will be necessary if you say:

"Oh, I am so inconsistent! How can I ask her to kiss a person she doesn't know when in a few years I'll be telling her not to talk to strangers?"

Magazine Advice

The following nuggets are mined from an article entitled "First Impressions Count" in a recent issue of the magazine *How to be a Popular Grandparent:*

Avoid wild, woolly, and excessive hair. Also, walrus mustaches and horsehair eyebrows.

Avoid eating fish, onions, and any other food that causes nose-wrinkling reactions.

Avoid jewelry that leaves indentations and bruises on young skin.

Avoid snapping dentures, loud laughs, and raucous, uncontrolled, and generally manic behavior.

Helpful Hint
You may understand their antics, but that doesn't mean you approve of them.

Questionnaire for Grandmothers

(To rate yourself as a grandmother, give one answer in each category and consult the numerical equivalent of each answer below and on the following page.)

1. When you met the newborn grandchild, was your first thought,
   (a) I'll help bring her up.____
   (b) No thanks. I've just finished raising my own.____
   (c) I'm experienced, I'd better take over.____

2. Do you think the way your mother taught you to look after your children is the only right way? Be honest. (a) Yes____
   (b) No____
   or
   (c) You attend child behavioral symposiums and read psychologists' columns.____
   or
   (d) You stand back and let the parents experiment on their own.____

3. How would you describe your behavior toward your grandchildren?
   (a) Cautious?____ (b) Nervous?____ (c) Possessive?____
   or
   (d) Indifferent?____ (e) Incompetent?____ (f) Devil-may-care?____
   or
   (g) Loving?____ (h) Spoiling?____ (i) Gushing?____ (j) Fawning?____

4. How would you be willing to help when they're having teenage problems?
   (a) Giving advice____ (b) Listening to them____ (c) Criticizing____

Quiz Answers

1. a=8; b=2; c=1.
2. a=2; b=6; c=4; d=8.
3. a=4; b=6; c=2; d=2; e=2; f=1; g=8; h=4; i=4; j=2.
4. a=4; b=8; c=0.

Now, add up your points and rate yourself as a grandmother:

If you scored 35 or better	Good for you, Grandma.
25-34	An interesting approach, but are you giving your all?
20-24	Work on your confidence and learn to trust.
15-19	You're indulgent and haven't come to terms with the experience of letting them live their own lives.
10-14	Don't panic. Get advice.
9 and below	Forget it.

Helpful Hint

When a newly toilet-trained person asks you to close the bathroom door, you can be quite sure he's had an accident.

Wise Precaution

Shut your eyes when the parents are teaching the child to walk down stairs.

BALLOONS

Grandparents often talk to other grandparents about their grandchildren. But many talk even more to other grandparents about how their children bring up the grandchildren.

"You know the child's still in diapers?"

"We've been lucky, our daughter-in-law's quite fastidious."

"Of course, she has a girl and we all know girls are easier to train than boys. But the real trouble is, someone told our daughter that toilet training must never be forced, that it was at the root of so much dissatisfaction in the world today... that it maybe even bred terrorists..."

"Well, here's to your daughter if she wants to add to her work load."

2. Three to Five:
SMALL CHALLENGES

Even before the grandchild has mastered numbers, she has learned to press the "5" on her parents' pushbutton telephone. This opens the line to your house and makes possible many delightful conversations. Most sentences start with "Why?"... silence... and even more with "Why not?"

Undoubtedly there had been some incursions into the grandparents' daily routine.

"Do you think the grandchildren are becoming more demanding?" Grandpa asked. "Remember, I'll be working at home now."

"It's simply that we see them more often." Grandma keeps her eyes on her book.

"For instance, he won't say his prayers until I've stretched out on the floor and he can kneel on my back."

"Sometimes I wonder whether you ever learned anything about children!" She shuts her book sharply.

"I can't see myself always lying on the floor. I repeat, what about my work?"

"And what about my cooking classes?"

"And what about my art?"

"You must learn how to balance the two demands."

"Of course, you would have the answer for everything."

"You see, you never had to juggle two demands when ours were growing up."

"Now you're telling me I wasn't a good father."

"All I'm telling you is that it's going to get worse before it gets better."

• • • • •

It is very cozy to have a small person in bed with you in the morning, particularly because you know you can send her back to her parents should she become rambunctious or should you require more sleep. It is wise, however, to have an understanding with the parents beforehand: the grandchild must be dry when she joins you, and eating cookies in bed is forbidden.

• • • • •

Babysitting. You're looking forward to the visit of the little dynamo. Prepare yourself for your tour of duty by

composing yourself. Meditate. Your world is about to be turned upside down. Remove breakable objects on low tables... the ones you put back in place when your own children grew up.

• • • • •

Remember, if the child suddenly has a temper tantrum at bedtime, it might be your fault for disturbing the order of things. Washing is done before teeth. Hair is combed after teeth. Then a story, tucking in, one last call for a glass of water. And finally, you hope, sleep.

• • • • •

Be prepared for a whole comedy of manners when you visit the granddaughter because it's usually she who visits you. Querying looks: What are you doing here? You don't belong in my house. She'll circle around you and after a while she'll take you into her bedroom and show you her toys. Meaning you've passed the test.

Then, when she visits you, she arrives round-eyed, excited but shy, reverting to incomprehensible baby talk — to her parents' embarrassment — finally feeling comfortable as she becomes aware of where she is.

This procedure is over sooner if you let her be.

• • • • •

An experienced grandparent will know how to distinguish between different ways of crying.

The fake cry: Stop reading your book, I'm bored.

Hurt feelings: How can you be so mean to someone who's smaller than you?

Embarrassment: You should have stopped me falling down in front of all those people.

Tearless roar: Why don't these two *Lego* pieces fit together?

Temper: I'll keep this up until you give me a popsicle.

The cry of pain: Grandma!

This is the one that makes you come running.

• • • • •

> Q. Who was the first Beatle to become a grandfather?
> A. Ringo Starr.

The Bond Between Generations

There is undoubtedly a bond between very small children and their grandparents that misses the middle generation:

the slowness of walk...

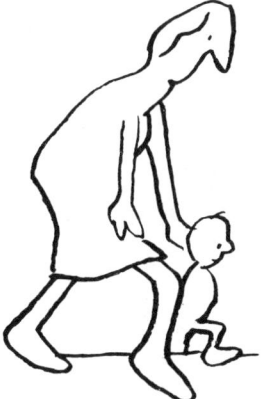

the unsureness of footing...

the searching for words...

the close appraisal of strangers...

the impatience...

the willfulness...

the need to be silly...

the need to cry...

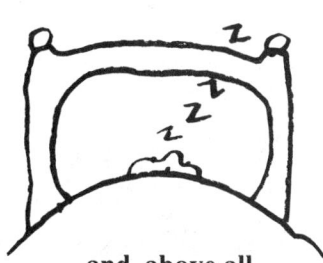

and, above all, the need to sleep.

One likes to assume that one's grandchild is born with a sense of humor. In order not to leave this to chance one should expose the child to jokes, antics, and gentle teasing.

However, you are somewhat taken aback when you find yourself laughing at your own efforts to be amusing and your grandchild says stonily, "That wasn't a funny joke."

You ask why not.

"Because I didn't laugh!"

• • • • •

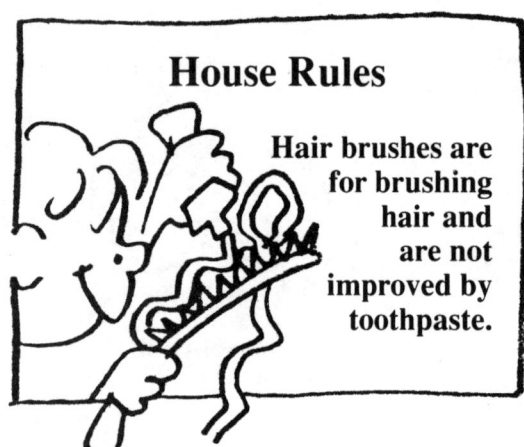

House Rules

Hair brushes are for brushing hair and are not improved by toothpaste.

The grandparent is assuring the child that the latter's move to the country doesn't mean they'll never see each other again.

Grandparent: I'll be there as soon as I can.

Grandchild: You come, and I'll show you everything.

Grandparent: I'll hold onto your dress so I can follow you.

Grandchild: I might not be wearing a dress.

Grandparent: I'll hold onto your hair

then. Surely you'll be wearing that?

Grandchild: Oh, yes, I even sleep in my hair.

• • • • •

It's a raw, windy day, but a watery sun has broken through the clouds for what seems like the first time in months. There's a hint of spring in the air. Young and old alike breathe a sigh of relief. The youngest grandchild comes out of the house. She glances at the sky, throws out her arms. "It's the sun!" she says. Eyeing you surreptitiously, she slips off her coat and begins to dance. So what if she does catch cold? Is it for you to stop this ancient ritual?

(continued on page 28)

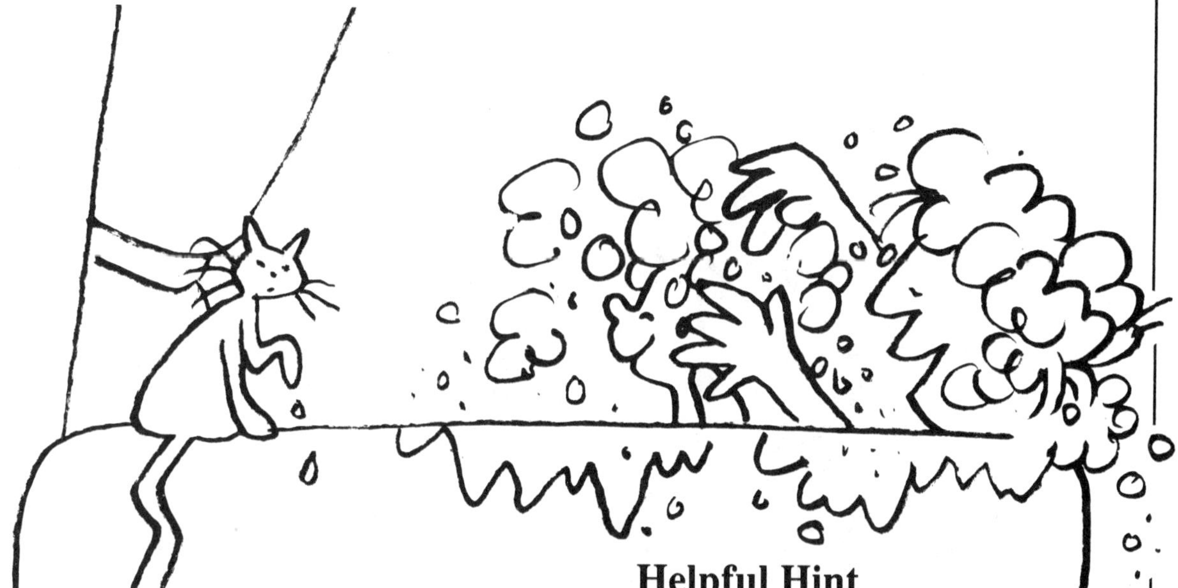

Helpful Hint

To forestall a tantrum at hair washing time, take the little one into the bath with you and wash each other's hair. Comb out each other's snarls, too.

At the end of the dance, she sits down on the still unthawed ground. Pneumonia, you worry, and just as you are about to suggest... she gets up. "I'm cold," she says, and brings her coat for you to put around her.

And when the same four-year-old in the heat of summer slips eel-like out of her clothes and rolls in the dust beside the cat, you can only feel wistful.

• • • • •

Wise Precaution
Every morning go out together and choose two flowers to pick. The rest are for sniffing.

Q. What was the name of Little Lord Fauntleroy's grandfather?

A. Lord Dorincourt.

• • • • •

In a public place a well-meaning stranger might pat your grandchild on the head, causing the little one to react, saying: "You're crowding me." Since the stranger is offended, your instinct is to chastize the child. Don't!

Having been warned about strangers, how can he be expected to differentiate between the good and the bad? You could teach him to whisper his comments, because fear must out... but, best of all, try not to put him in the position of having to defend himself, just whisk him away before he feels the need.

• • • • •

It was your week to take your grandson to nursery school and on Monday one of his classmates appeared wearing a pair of pink plastic shoes. She immediately became the star attraction. By the middle of the week many of the little girls were sporting similar pairs and the grandson grew quieter and quieter.

"What's the matter?" you ask, although you have an uncomfortable suspicion. Sure enough.

"Please, will you buy me a pair of pink shoes," he begs.

Well, why not? Boys play with dolls these days, don't they? So — "Of course," you tell him. Then you picture your son-in-law's reaction.

"But on the condition that you only wear them in school."

Helpful Hint

You may have forgotten that hiding means putting fingers in front of the face and peeping through them.

• • • • •

It is futile to try to keep the child out of your garden. You can set aside a miniature plot close by and plant it with easily tended herbs and a few pansies. You can call it "your garden." But for the children the pleasure comes from digging in the real garden right beside you. Don't be selfish. Let them be part of the planning and planting of the garden, too — if you want help with the raking and weeding later. Anyway, "Let's do it together" is always considered more entertaining, whether it be gardening or crayoning or taking a nap. As they advance in years, grandparents, too, enjoy doing things together.

My Italian Grandparents

My grandfather was first a cavalryman and then a lawyer from Rome who settled in Newark, New Jersey. My grandmother was of a different background, from Naples. Nevertheless, when my grandfather wanted to marry my grandmother, her father disapproved. Impassioned, my grandfather shot himself and carried the bullet over his heart for the rest of his life. "Can I feel it?" I, as his granddaughter, often wanted to ask. But this was not a permissible question to ask a stern old man.

Every single night before his large dinner he would have two, just two, martinis, and little crackers with anchovies on top.

And when there was a pie for dessert, he'd always take his fork, cut off the tip, and push it to the side of his plate. Nobody ever asked him why, but we still wonder.

SANDRA SCOPPETTONE

Picnic Menus

In these days of working parents and working grandmothers, a retired grandfather is often asked to babysit. "Meals are something we'll learn to make ourselves," he told his grandson. "A balanced diet is so important," said Grandmother.

After a few days of sitting in the kitchen, eating hardboiled eggs, celery sticks, and burned toast, they decided to take their meals to the park. So they went to the supermarket and mapped out menus for the week as follows:

MENU #3
Spam
Kraft's processed cheese
Potato chips
Chip-A-Roos
Peanuts

MENU #1
Chunky Chicken Nibbles
Fritos
Mallopuffs
Peanuts

MENU #4
Peanut butter
Puffed Cheez Doodles
Peanut butter cups
Fluff
Peanuts

MENU #2
Tuna fish
Pretzel log "pushers"
Popcorn
Cookies'n Fudge Bars
Peanuts

MENU #5
Vienna sausages
Doritos
Ice'n Creamy Freezer Snack
Peanuts

One recognizes the character changes that occur when the oldest grandchild goes to school. Apart from her ABC's, she now spends time jockeying for position and learning expressions like: "I hate you." "Me first." "It's mine." "I won't be your friend." And, sadly, becoming aware of the baser instincts.

• • • • •

A telephone conversation.

"Grandpa, my gerbil..."

The breathless little voice, lips touching the phone, makes the rest hard to unscramble, so Grandpa fills in the pause by laughing.

"Why are you laughing, Grandpa?"

"Well, I thought it was one of your jokes."

"But I was telling you my gerbil's sick."

The phone is thrown down, and Grandpa hears her say, "Grandpa's laughing because my gerbil's sick. That's not very kind, is it, Daddy?"

And then her father's voice: "Oh, forget it, Grandpa's always had a thing about gerbils."

Grandpa hangs up. It's too embarrassing to have to explain about his deafness.

• • • • •

On TV, even the classic *Wizard of Oz* can produce a lot of scared talk around Halloween.

Grandchild: "Grandpa, Grandpa, there's a witch in the closet."

Grandpa looks skeptical.

"No, no. Grandpa, there really is, I saw her." The grandchild climbs onto his lap, her eyes rolling.

"Don't be daft, that's Grandma in the closet."

"Grandma doesn't have hair like that."

"She's taken her hair down, getting ready for bed."

"Can't be Grandma. No, it's not true."

"Neither are witches."

• • • • •

Helpful Hint

Personal remarks about other people should be whispered in your ear and passed upon by you before being spoken out loud.

Ellen and the V. P.

My granddaughter, Ellen Stuart, paid us a visit in Washington when she was four years old. Ellen is one of those children who love everybody.

During her visit, the White House called Mrs. Helms and invited her to attend the arrival ceremony for a visiting head of state.

About two hundred people gathered and lined up on two sides of the Rose Garden. Vice President Bush and Mrs. Bush took their places on the other side.

Mrs. Helms was engaged in conversation with other Senate wives and suddenly noticed that Ellen had vanished. Anxiously she looked around and finally spotted her.

Ellen was on the other side with her arms around the Vice President's legs. She had seen him on television many times and decided to go across the Rose Garden to greet him.

SENATOR JESSE HELMS

It is hard to know what the home rules are. Last year if you had refused to buy your grandchild a package of Hostess Twinkies, she would have burst into noisy tears in the store. This year she looks you straight in the eye saying, "Mother lets me." You really don't know whether to believe her. But you give in.

On the other hand, when you are walking down the street and she tries to slip her hand out of yours, again saying, "Mother lets me," you know that's a lie.

• • • • •

The grandchild is crying as the mother leaves. To comfort her, you say, "Why do you cry when your mother goes out? She'll be back."

"I cry when she goes to parties because I think she likes parties better than me."

As the grandparent, you may be able to find out what's wrong, but what can be done about it is now strictly a matter between mother and child.

• • • • •

The father is teaching his daughter how to lace her sneakers. "In one window," he says. "Out the next."

She concentrates ferociously, and they both laugh.

The grandfather watches with interest.

"I don't remember ever sitting down and teaching you to thread your shoelaces. Looks like you're having fun."

"Yeah, we are. Why didn't you?"

"I guess I didn't dare, because in those days I'd have been the only male mother in my neighborhood."

• • • • •

If you're having guests for dinner, don't panic. Remember, you have a built-in *sous-chef*. Place her up on the counter (so that instead of hanging around your knees she can see what's happening) and get to work.

Make sure you serve string beans on such occasions. Beans produce a satisfying snap and take a nice, long time. When that becomes boring, "cleaning the bathroom" can be a popular pastime, and it frees you to concentrate on recipes; but make sure sand castles aren't being made out of the soap powder or your toothbrush used to clean the sink.

On Mistakes Grandparents Make

Dr. Rose Dobrof, Brookdale Professor of Gerontology at Hunter College, and Executive Director of the Brookdale Center on Aging, offers the following observations on common mistakes grandparents make:

Interference. Non-interference is the main thing for grandparents to practice. Do not give unsolicited advice. Smart grandparents abide by the rules of their children. Let the parents mediate the relationship between grandparents and grandchildren. It should be the parents' choice as to when the grandparents see the grandchildren and when they should not.

Overprotection. You're scared to death. God forbid that something should happen to the grandchildren while they are in your care.

Overfeeding. Nutritional standards differ between your generation and that of your children.

Bribing. Of course, one bribes them all the time.

Playing favorites. Favoritism can be very painful and can cause great tension in the family. Grandparents may favor the grandchildren of a favorite child. It is wrong to play these kinds of intra-family games.

You and your grandson share a fondness for peanuts, but there comes a time when even you have had enough, and you put them out of temptation on a high shelf. After a moment, the grandson asks if he should pass them again. "I'm hungry," he explains.

"Hungry!" you say. "We've already eaten half the jar."

"I'd carry them over to you except I can't reach."

"Nor can I."

"Yes, you can. You just put them there."

Caught in his lie, Grandpa succumbs.

• • • • •

Or there was the time, at your house, when you'd both been polishing off a plate of Walker's Pure Butter Shortbread and now only one piece remains. You look at each other. Then the child leans forward, repeating the rule he has been taught when his friends come visiting. "Mother says guests must always take first," he tells you earnestly, reaching for the cookie.

• • • • •

You're being fanciful if you think you're the one to teach your grandchild to ride a bike. Could you have forgotten how hard it was with your own children? It's tiring enough at the wobbly stage, but suddenly the cyclist catches on, and off you go.

You are running flat out, your lungs are bursting, your heart is pounding. "Stop, use the brake," you say, gasping. He laughs with the sheer power of it.

"Let me go!" he shouts. You cannot let go. You must return him to his parents in the condition in which he was given to you. Just as you are about to expire, the front wheel turns sharply off the sidewalk and you both tumble onto the grass.

He jumps up. "Let's do it again!" You continue to lie for a while, thinking, if you'd been my own child, I would have let go.

• • • • •

"Let's do it again!"

Family Quiz

In each of the following professions, the grandparent, the parent in between, and the grandchild, won fame: early American politics, classical music, later American politics, and the movies. The initial letters of the families involved were, in order, A, B, T, and H. Can you name the families and the individuals in the three generations?

Quiz Answers

Answers to family quiz (grandparent, parent in between, and grandchild): "A" — John Adams, John Quincy Adams, Charles Francis Adams; "B" — Johann Sebastian Bach, Johann Christoph Friedrich Bach, Wilhelm Friedrich Ernst Bach; "T" — William Howard Taft, Robert A. Taft, Robert Taft, Jr.; "H" — Walter Huston, John Huston, Anjelica Huston.

My grandfather found his grandchild's fogbound solitudes sweeter than human society.

Life Studies
"Dunbarton"
ROBERT LOWELL

You turned your head for a minute and the five-year-old is up on the trampoline. He's ecstatic. But suppose he has an accident while you're in charge. How to get him off? You coax, you threaten, you even try a usually surefire bribe, "Grandma's making brownies tonight, and you can lick the beaters." But he's laughing so much he doesn't even hear.

Well, there's nothing to do but to get up there yourself. You find you can't stand. He watches. Frustrated, you bounce on your knees, and suddenly you bounce so high you can straighten your legs. You're airborne! Fifty-four years old and you've licked the trampoline. You, too, are ecstatic as you and your grandson bounce side by side.

• • • • •

Her parents gave her a blue jacket just before they left. "Wear this," they said, "and you won't be lonely when we're away."

The grandchild stands in the doorway, a tiny figure in her blue jacket. The parents wave. She lifts her hand.

"They'll be back soon," you tell her. "Soon."

She doesn't know what "soon" is.

"A day or two after you wake up," you say. "Shall I read you a story?"

She shrugs her shoulders. "Can I sleep in your bed tonight?"

We look at each other, both remembering this is a practice her parents discourage. But how can you disappoint her on this day?

"Yes," you tell her. "Tonight."

She breaks into a little jig. "Tonight in my blue jacket?"

• • • • •

On seeing a nun boarding a bus, you should not wince when you hear your grandchild ask piercingly, "Is she a witch? Is she going to a Halloween party?"

"Shh..." you say.

Nor should you feel embarrassed

Wise Precaution

Ask kindly after the other grandparents. Mask your disappointment when you hear that, despite all your efforts, it is they who have succeeded in teaching the grandchild how to write his name.

Wise Precaution

Never let them see where you pick the raspberries.

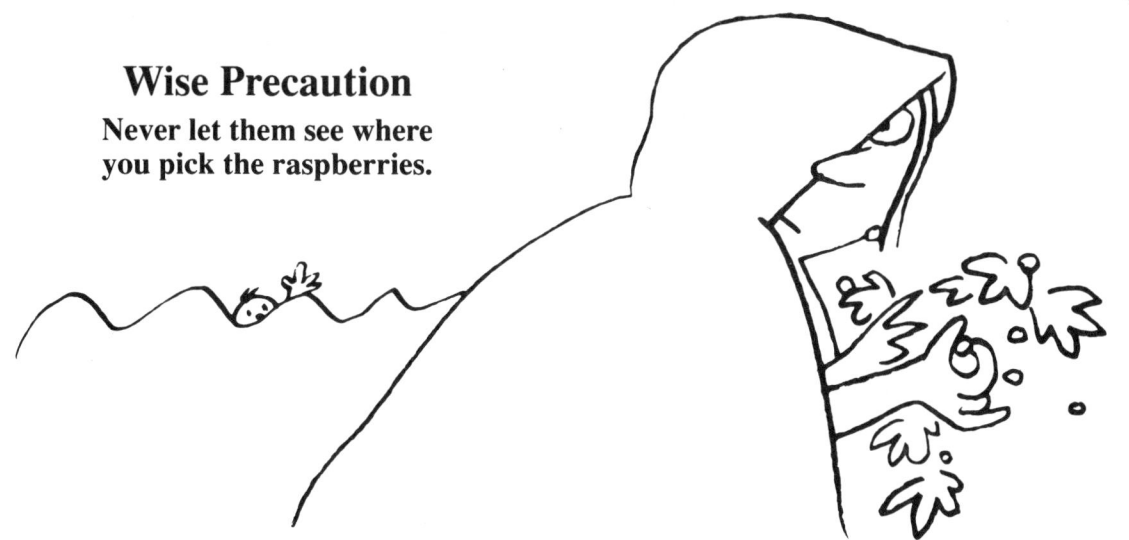

when another grandchild notices a dark baby and announces loudly: "Look, Grandma, that baby has a brown face." Remember the reverse situation when a little black boy peered into your grandchild's carriage and told his grandmother, "Look, Grandma! It's a baby Jesus!"

• • • • •

Our son Jeffrey called collect from Sweden to his home in California.

Our five-year-old grandson, Aaron, answered the phone.

Jeff heard the overseas operator say, "I have a collect phone call from Jeffrey Parks. Will you accept charges?"

Aaron sighed and said, "Okay, I'll take it, but I don't have any money!"

BERT PARKS

My grandmother took me out in a canoe at night and taught me astronomy and Greek. —LEE STARR

"How can she see through her back?"

This time the grandmother is having a business discussion on the phone. She is somewhat distracted by the sight of her grandson circling a forbidden piece of cake. She can see his mind working. "Will she notice? No, her back's turned. I'll try it." His hand snakes out.

"Just a minute," the grandmother says into the phone. The child jumps.

She turns. "Did you really think that because I was talking I wouldn't notice you helping yourself to that cake?"

Darn it, he thinks. How can she see through her back?

Your five-year-old granddaughter is showing you her newborn baby brother. "It's a boy," she says enthusiastically, doubtless imitating the proud tones of her parents.

Then, pulling at your sleeve, she lowers her voice. "He's nothing but a little crumb, Grandma. Why don't you take him home with you?"

• • • • •

> The lamp, quivering and flaring up as though in fear of something, lighted up our cottage... and all of us children collected in a cluster, listened to our grandfather, who had not crawled off the stove for more than five years, owing to his great age.
>
> *St. John's Eve*
> NIKOLAI GOGOL

Here's a way to be sure they eat what's good for them. It is eight o'clock and time for breakfast with your three-year-old grandchild. "Fried eggs?" you ask.

Attempting to overcome your morning inertia, you make a feeble joke.

"Fri-ed eggs on Fri-days?"

"No," says the grandson. "I want watermelon."

"Please."

"Please."

Well, watermelon won't harm anyone, you think, as you give him a slice at the table. Then you prepare your own fried eggs and a cup of coffee. And with the newspaper in your free hand, you get ready for the first relaxed moment of the day. A head appears from beneath the newspaper.

"What's that on your plate?" he asks.

"Fried eggs. You didn't want any."

He pulls himself up onto your lap. "I do now."

"Well, take a mouthful. I want to read the paper."

• • • • •

You can easily understand why your grandson likes hugging the puppy tightly. Letting its legs drag, its head loll. How many living bodies are small enough for him to lift and are furry and squeezable, to boot? But on your way to rescue the poor animal you stop yourself, suddenly remembering the countless puppies that have survived being squeezed by countless generations of children, yourself included. Besides, the puppy seems to like it.

• • • • •

Little children like to give their "best friend" something pretty. Grandmother, seeing her wedding ring on a small boy's thumb, takes her granddaughter aside:

Grandmother: Why, that's mine, where did you find it?

Granddaughter: I found it in my crayon box.

Grandmother: Really? I think you'd better let me have it now.

Granddaughter: I can't give it to you. We're married.

Helpful Hint
See if you can be the first grandparent to teach a three-year-old to blow his nose.

Dressing the reluctant granddaughter can be a challenge. Having discarded her overalls, and hidden them behind the refrigerator, she has planted herself on the sofa, all thirty-five pounds of her, and is sitting on her feet, pillows stacked on top, arms crossed, wearing an expression of triumphant cunning.

"Now, dear, nobody goes to pre-nursery school without their clothes."

She shakes her head mutely.

Getting the overalls on this time is obviously going to be a two-grandparent operation. One of you picks up the crayons and begins to draw, diverting attention, as the other manages to dress her.

The maneuver has been successful, yes. But take heed. As the child becomes more knowing, one must continually think up new distractions.

• • • • •

Q. Who was the grandson of the Duke of Greystone?
A. uɐzɹɐꞱ

BALLOONS

3. Six to Eight:
AHEAD OF THE (CON) GAME

A grandparent's nose might become slightly out of joint, as the child begins to seek outside companionship. Yes, he is preparing to ditch you. However, you know from experience that he will still accept an occasional cuddle. Walk carefully. Many small traps are being laid for the unwary. You might try laying some traps of your own.

One early morning the grandfather goes into his study. He is dressed in his bathrobe and carries a cup of coffee that spills into the saucer. The grandmother follows warily.

"How can I run my business from home?" he asks. "It's just like I thought. How can I concentrate with the grandchildren running in every other minute, asking for a dollar for this, a dollar for that?"

"It's not the interruptions that disturb you, it's the fact that they want you to give them money for nothing. You should assign jobs, make them earn it," the grandmother suggests.

"They laugh when I give them something to do. They like seeing how much they can get away with."

"Just testing their wings."

"And my patience. They should know someone had to work hard to make all this (he waves his arm) possible for them."

"They know you as Grandpa, for Heaven's sake, not as the family provider. When they're older they'll connect the two and understand."

"Listen, if they're old enough to know

who has the dollar bills, they're old enough to know how they happened to be in that person's pocket."

• • • • •

You are getting the granddaughters ready for a special occasion, but by the time you've dressed yourself the boisterous one needs dressing all over again.

She's been galloping around the room, jumping up and down on the bed, pushing at her sister, who prefers to sit quietly admiring herself in the mirror.

"Oh, do simmer down," you say, placing the wriggler firmly in a chair. "Look at your crumpled dress, and your hair's like a rat's nest and your socks have already gone to sleep in your shoes. Can't you ever be still?"

"I'm going to a party," she shouts. "Ice cream and cake and my friends."

"I've got a good mind not to take you, the way you're behaving."

"Please, please, I'll be good."

"Dress me first," says her sister, Little Miss Prim, forcing herself away from the mirror. "And dress her last, so she doesn't have time to get untidy."

"I really don't need your advice," you say.

She sniffs, hurt. Her sister comes to the rescue.

"She's only trying to help, Grandma," she says. "You're just cross because you didn't think of it yourself!"

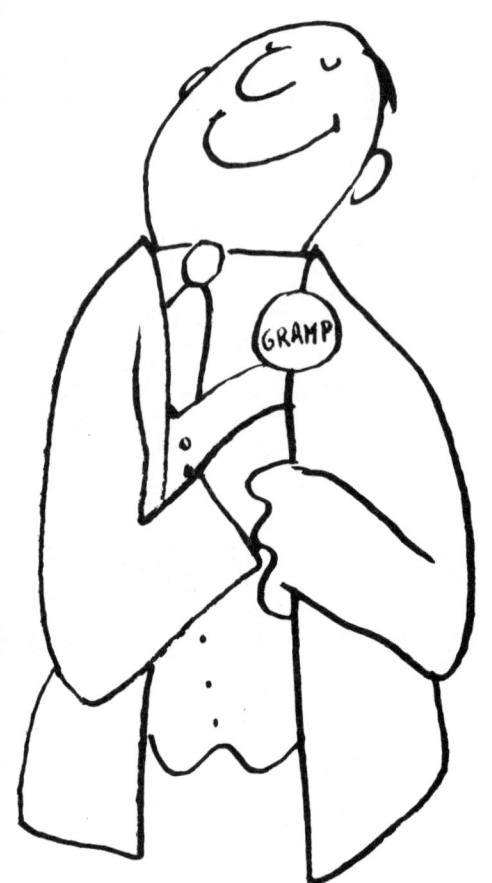

Political wisdom notwithstanding, grandfatherhood is indeed the only bonafide, goldplated, truly authentic "free lunch."

I am adored, revered, honored, and very often idolized for doing exactly nothing. It is my greatest accomplishment, and I am exhausted.

JAMES WHITMORE

• • • • •

Helpful Hint

Make a point of discussing family plans with your grandchildren, but don't forget to tell them when the program changes.

Grandparents have to recognize that the grandchildren have an instinctive interest in money, even before they know what it really means. So it is not surprising to see a six-year-old, on awakening, reach under his bed, bring out a tin adorned with a couple of cavorting butterflies, and start counting his loot like an embryonic Midas. Though, who knows, he might become a philanthropist instead.

• • • • •

Generations of children have been tempted by loose change left on the bureau, and you enter as your grandson's chubby fingers deposit some pennies into his open butterfly tin. It is obvious he knows you have seen him, because he puts the guilty hand behind his back.

Looking at the remaining change, silently, you turn to face him.

"Gracious me," you say. "I seem to be missing four cents. Would you mind if I took them out of your tin?"

His face is a study.

• • • • •

Introduction to the Theater

Grandpa: I have a surprise. You and I are going to the theater this afternoon.

Granddaughter: Willie wants to come over.

Grandma: We'll ask Willie tomorrow. (aside to Grandpa) Perhaps you should have told her before.

Grandpa (aside to Grandma): Then it wouldn't be a surprise.

Granddaughter: I don't want a surprise. I want to see Willie.

After lunch, Grandpa helps her into her snowsuit and ties on her woolly hat.

"Enjoy yourselves," says Grandma, looking forward to an afternoon alone with her book.

At six o'clock they are home. The child races into the living room. She throws her legs across the easy chair, eyes sparkling, hat askew.

"It was the bestest theater I ever saw," she shouts.

House Rule
Television shouldn't be considered an acceptable substitute for your attention.

*Try not to smile when the parents proudly explain that *their* child has an iron will. *Every* child has an iron will.*

Don't leave the hors d'oeuvres unattended while you dress for the party or you may find the young ones have had a field day. There will be little teeth marks in the olives, a discarded mouthful of blue cheese on a plate, and finger holes in the pâté. But what can you really expect when you leave so much food in plain sight?... As the party moves into top gear, and the guests have stopped talking to the grandchildren, the little dears must find other ways to entertain themselves, like blowing ashes out of the ash trays or fiddling with the gas stove.

• • • • •

"Grandma, can Honey stay for lunch?" she asks.

You agree because you don't feel you can say "no" with Honey standing in front of you. Afterwards, you tell your granddaughter, "I don't mind your asking someone for a meal, but please don't do it so she can hear, in case there isn't enough food, or whatever."

She agrees. So the next time Honey comes, your granddaughter whispers the request in your ear with many a glance at her friend, obviously in on the secret.

• • • • •

Helpful Hint

Don't leave money lying around. Even if your grandchild isn't thinking in terms of stealing (Heaven help us!), he might be thinking in terms of "borrowing."

Show enthusiasm when your grandchild has succeeded in fashioning a bread carving board shaped like a fish in carpentry class. But don't overdo it in front of the other children. There's a whole display of carving boards shaped like fish. Wait until you get home to smother the child with kisses. • • • • •

Some hopeful grandparents try to develop independent thinking in the grandchild. This particular grandparent thought a lecture on Fagin's role in *Oliver Twist* might warn the child about peer pressure. And, encouraged by his rapt expression, asked:

"What were you thinking about during the talk, dear?"

"What?" said the grandson.

"You looked so far away."

"Oh, I was thinking about whether I'd have a hot dog or hamburger for lunch."

• • • • •

Avoid getting caught in the middle of a parent-to-child quarrel.

Child to parent: Grandpa said I needn't wear my boots today, didn't you, Grandpa?

Mother: Really, Grandpa, how could you? There must be two inches of snow out there.

Grandpa to child: You never told me it was snowing.

Child: I did, I did.

(The grandfather keeps silent, although he knows who is telling the truth. Later, of course . . .)

Mother to Grandpa: You make everything so hard when you interfere.

A Grandparent's Christmas List

Dear Santa:
Please send a pair of hands to find my glasses and another pair to find my needlecase and then a pair of eyes to thread the needle. One strong wrist to unscrew my vitamin bottle. A memory to tell me what I said to my son-in-law yesterday to make him so cold toward me today.

Please trim my stomach so I need not fear a rupture when I put on my overshoes, and restore the elasticity of my waist to enable me to cut the corners of my toenails without making unseemly guttural sounds. Please give me the brains to get the conversation back where it was when I forgot where I was, and the ability to remember the name as well as the face.

Thank you, Santa, but please hurry.

Helpful Hint
Never talk down to your grandchildren.

• • • • •

He's the youngest of five and his mother is tired of fights and confrontations, so when he's troublesome she simply leaves him in the hands of a brother or sister.

He bounces on the sofa filling his mouth with six grapes simultaneously.

"Stop bouncing," his mother says for the fifth time. He spits out grape seeds and, as before, he ignores her. "All right, I'm going to the supermarket."

"What's it to you," he shouts as she leaves. "You're always going out." He gets off the sofa, slowly, looking small and defeated.

Grandmother feels it is time to step in.

"Why don't you let me handle this," she tells her daughter.

"I'd be grateful, I don't seem to be able to face these confrontations anymore."

Looking at him, the grandmother begins, "You'd never dare talk to me that way."

"Because you'd never let me."

"So you do know you shouldn't be rude to your mother?"

"She can't stop me."

"Could be she goes out so she doesn't have to listen to you."

"What? You mean if I wasn't a pain, she'd stay?"

"Try it."

• • • • •

Biblical Quiz

The first column is list of grandchildren found in the Bible. The second column consists of grandparents. Match the names in the first column with their grandparents in the second column.

a. Ephraim	1. Laban
b. Noah	2. Obed
c. Reuben	3. Boaz
d. Esau	4. Ham
e. Joseph	5. Jacob
f. David	6. Isaac
g. Enoch	7. Herod the Great
h. Solomon	8. Jesse
i. Jesse	9. Methuselah
j. Nimrod	10. Eve
k. Canaan	11. Sarah
l. Salome	12. Noah

Answers:

a-5; b-9; c-1; d-11; e-6; f-2; g-10; h-8; i-3; j-4; k-12; l-7

Wise Precaution

Find a hiding place for your favorite candy. And don't feel bad about holding out on the grandchildren. You're protecting their teeth.

Wise Precaution

Who wants to be a second-generation corrections officer? Before you say "No," try to remember what you did at that age.

Helpful Hint

If the grandparents seem to have more patience than the parents, it is because the grandparents have more time. Grandparents often have the luxury of dealing with their grandchildren singly, whereas the parents deal collectively. This rules out a certain finesse and patience becomes the casualty.

• • • • •

Whatever your age, death is always an interesting subject. One child was constantly telling her grandparents they'd be dead in six months. She repeated this often enough for them to begin to worry. However, six months came and went. The oracle began to occupy herself with other prophecies, and the grandparents crept around, hoping to stay out of her visionary range.

• • • • •

Although it is barely light, noise is coming from the grandchildren's bedroom.

"What now?" you ask rather tersely.

"She bit me," the boy shouts.

"Because he sat on my face," the girl answered.

"I can't sleep when she turns the light on."

"I hate the dark. That's why we don't share a room at home."

You think a minute. "Let me tell you, when my brother and I visited our grandparents we weren't allowed to talk in bed and if we fought we'd be packed off home. Now, how would you like that?"

They look at each other.

"That's not . . . " one says.

" . . . funny," says the other.

"Quite correct," you say.

• • • • •

Wise Precaution
Ten minutes of complete and utter attention is more valuable than a whole morning of on-again off-again concentration.

Helpful Hint
To guard against endless interruptions, take a minute or two to listen to what the grandchild is trying to say. Then you have a perfect right to get on with the adult conversation.

• • • • •

Father: Aren't you going to give Grandpa a kiss?

Grandchild (backing up behind his father): His face tickles.

Father: Now, didn't I tell you to be a nice boy? Give Grandpa a kiss.

Grandchild (in a shrill whisper): He's always been eating something horrid.

Father (firmly): Grandpa says he might send you to college one day.

Grandchild: What's college?

Father: Just give Grandpa a kiss.

After the grandson had begged and begged for a fishing rod, eventually, of course, the grandparents relented.

"But no fishing off the end of the pier," they admonished. "The weight of the rod could pull you into the water, even without a fish."

The child obeyed for a week, until the day he discovered both grandparents napping. Immediately he was off to the pier and, naturally, he fell in. He was pulled out by a passerby, and watched his rod ride out to sea.

The grandparents agreed they would not punish him. He must have learned a lesson.

"When he brings the matter up, we'll point out the dangers."

But as the days went by and the child asked no questions, behaving, in fact, in his normal cheerful fashion, the grandparents began to worry.

"I can't understand why there's no sign of trauma," said Grandma, who'd had her share of therapy. The child looked away.

Grandma was exasperated. "You had to be scared. What did you think about all alone in the water after you fell off the pier?"

"That my fishing rod was floating away."

Later Grandpa said rather proudly, "That kid has plenty of guts."

"And he did learn a lesson, too," Grandma added. "He didn't beg for another fishing rod."

One parent is away, the other is sick, and suddenly you find you are giving the birthday party. Out comes the tablecloth. Maybe you should know better, but it's been a long time since you held a birthday party for an eight-year-old.

Grandpa sets the table, a job at which he believes he excels. Paper hats on the right side, noise-makers on the left, the first daffodils from the garden as a centerpiece. The birthday kid has been scrubbed and dressed for an hour or so. He cannot keep still. The guests arrive, early, with a mighty roar. They race around, bumping the table. There go the daffodils!

"All right," you say, "time to eat." The chicken salad is devoured in five minutes. Faces are red and shiny, paper hats askew. Bread pellets are flying through the air, balloons popping.

"All right," you say above the din of the noise-makers. "Time for dessert."

"Happy birthday!" they chorus as the cake is carried in. There's silence for a while, until the cake disappears, all but the frosting on their upper lips.

"All right," you say again. "Time for presents." Try not to notice that the box with your rather costly tweed jacket lies open but unmentioned. Now the wrapping paper is bunched up and used as a

(continued on next page)

football. Shirt tails have escaped from slacks. The party seems to be a success, you say, nodding to each other. The time has come when matters are so out of control all you can do is sit and watch.

Finally, the parents arrive, late, to collect their children. When they are all gone, in the sudden silence, you inspect the damage. The whole house is a disaster area. You pour yourselves drinks, sink into the sofa, and promise to clean up the next day.

• • • • •

My Polish Grandfather

We spent all our vacations with our grandparents. My grandfather was Tatar, high cheekbones, you know, and stiff-standing hair. My brother wanted to look like him so much that my mother would make his hair into spikes with sugar and water.

My grandfather was a cabinetmaker, every design created by hand, no machines. He would make toys for us, and we'd sit quietly all morning as the wood chips flew around us.

He seldom spoke, but would indicate when he wanted to go for a walk. Of course we followed. If we complained we were cold, he'd take our coats and open them, saying, "Arms back, chest forward, count to seven, breathe deeply, cold now is divided over all the body, you are warm."

And we always were.

ELZBIETA KIELAR

4. Nine to Twelve:

CHANGE THE SUBJECT BEFORE YOU LOSE THE ARGUMENT

They may be, and often are, argumentative, fresh, and brutally frank, trying to see just how much leeway they are allowed. If this behavior is taken lightly, it becomes less burdensome. They are also beginning to question the universe, which might lead to more philosophical discussions.

One evening the grandparents were sitting in front of the fire, resting after a strenuous day with the young ones. It wasn't that they minded pulling an occasional oar on the family crew. It was simply that they became quite fatigued when they also had to be captain and mate.

"Of course we don't have them all and every day," she said.

"Feels like it sometimes."

"And they do save the more serious problems for their parents..." she replied, pursuing her own line of thought.

"It's drive, drive, drive everywhere. Cooking classes, ballet school, fencing lessons. Sometimes I'm so stiff I can hardly get out of the car."

"True, if they're old enough for fencing lessons, they could get there by bike. We must take a stand."

"But how can you take a stand when they're so beguiling?"

"Oh, let's enjoy them. They'll be grown before we know it."

A Boy of Eleven

No father was prouder, however, than when his son, at school, at church, at a picnic, or anywhere, got up and made a speech.

"The boy!" the father would shout at his eighty-eight-year-old father. "Listen to him! It's Vahan, my son, your grandson — eleven years old. He's talking about Europe."

The grandfather would shake his head and wonder what it was all about, a boy of eleven so serious and so well-informed, talking about Europe.

The old man scarcely would know where Europe was, although he would know he had visited Havre on his way to America. Perhaps Havre — perhaps that was Jevroba. Europe.

My Name Is Aram
WILLIAM SAROYAN

No sane grandparent would join a game of hide and seek or repetitive games such as War, Go Fish, and Pick Up Sticks.

However, introducing the grandchildren to games of skill for small stakes can be very productive. Their natural inclinations are cutthroat and mean. They mangle the cards and resort to pushing and cries of: "She cheated, she had another trump," or "He knows because he looked at my hand. That's cheating, too, isn't it, Grandpa?"

Gradually, through an example of patience and perseverance, they learn that winning honestly is as great an achievement as cheating (though maybe not quite as lucrative). It's better to expose them to good sportsmanship before they meet coaches and real competition.

• • • • •

Helpful Hint
Let them explain before you censure.

The grandfather is at his desk having a difficult time balancing his checkbook.

However, his grandson is in the mood for conversation.

Grandson: Are you going to die soon, Grandpa?

Grandpa: Oh, I don't know. I hadn't really thought about it. (To himself) Why doesn't this add up?

Grandson: Why do you have to die?

Grandpa: Sooner or later we all must.

Grandson: But why?

Grandpa, putting down his pen: Well, I suppose you get old and you go to sleep and you don't want to get up anymore.

Grandson: And you'd be put in the ground and I'd never see you again.

Grandpa, getting up and flexing his muscles: I haven't gone yet. Race you to the end of the road.

A child's illness can be very violent and sometimes, happily, very brief. There is a touch of drama in many of us and one day Gran gets an urgent, whispered call from her daughter.

Gran arrives as soon as possible and finds an anxious mother, pacing with a thermometer.

"What shall I do, Mother?"

Experienced in the illnesses of children, Gran is calm. "Nothing much you can do except keep her quiet. Call the doctor if she isn't better tomorrow. You'll know. Children don't fake illness."

Gran looks at the flushed face and closed eyes and hopes her experience won't desert her.

The next day she hurries back and can see at a glance that the child is much improved, though still lying listlessly, like

(continued on next page)

Little White Lies

The grandchildren were enjoying a pillow fight—bound to end in tears, you think, and before you can stop them, the youngest gets (accidentally?) slugged by his sister, causing a nosebleed and, as expected, tears.

The boy was invited to a friend's house that afternoon, but looking at his rapidly swelling nose, you feel you must cancel the date. Over his howls, you telephone.

"... so sorry he can't come today. He had a little accident.... no, Heavens no, just run of the mill, nothing serious..."

"Why didn't you say I hit him?" asked the girl.

"Surely you don't want everyone to know how we behave at home? Besides, a good excuse doesn't offend anyone."

"You're always telling us not to lie."

"That wasn't a lie, it's just better not to let on that we go around hitting each other. Some things are best kept in the family."

"Whichever way, Grandma," the voice drones on inexorably, "you were not telling the truth."

"Well, it was a fabrication, yes, which is also called a social lie, and that's quite different."

You look into her uncomprehending eyes and suddenly understand.

"Yes, why didn't I simply say you hit him? All children hit each other," you tell her. "Maybe I'd better stop telling social lies."

(continued from page 59)
the Lady of the Camellias.

"Glad to see you are better today. Yesterday you were terribly sick."

"Yes, I was terribly sick."

"When I saw you on the sofa with your head hanging down, I was worried."

"Oh, Gran, I was gone, really gone."

"Think you could manage a game of Hearts, or are you still too weak?"

The invalid gets up and fetches the cards. "Five cents a game," she says.

● ● ● ● ●

Some mad message from his mad grandfather.

Titus Andronicus ACT IV, SC. 2, LINE 3

One grandson is a cause of distress at mealtimes. He spills his milk, leaves a jammy knife on the table, puts his face in the cereal bowl and licks it for the last trace of sugar. So when a friend asks him for lunch, you send him off with severe misgivings.

Some days later, you run into this friend's mother. She describes your grandson's beautiful table manners, how he put his plate in the dishwasher and even offered to sponge off the table. She hopes her own son will learn something from this behavior.

"Beautiful table manners," you mutter, and you ask your grandson why on earth he doesn't practice them at home.

"But at home I know you like me anyway," he says.

• • • • •

Grandparent: And what are your other grandparents growing in the garden this year?

Grandchild: Not so many weeds. Of course, they have a gardener. (Tactfully sensing his grandparent's chagrin) O.K. I'll do some weeding for you tomorrow if you'll drive me to miniature golf.

Fact File

The rolls of the National Campers and Hikers Association include approximately 6,000 grandparents, about 25 percent of the membership.

• • • • •

Helpful Hint

Treat your grandchildren politely in the hope that they will return the compliment.

My Filipino Grandfather

My brother and I used to go into the swamps and for our sling gun make bullets out of the fruit of the swamp trees. Shooting away, we would forget mealtime and then my grandfather would take his slipper (he had a very large foot) and smack us. The more we cried, the more he smacked. Ten times or so.

Once before, we were late for a meal because we were playing with the tops we had made (a wooden top with a nail placed in the end and a string attached). My grandfather boiled the tops and said, "Next time I'll boil up the nails."

Another time, my art teacher asked me to make a picture. I refused. He said, "Then you can't come to any classes." So I played outside the school and my brother saw me and told my grandfather. My grandfather, who was the town's treasurer and disbursed the money for the school, went to the art teacher and said, "What is this about a picture? Don't you realize it's more important for this boy to be learning his lessons than making some picture?"

The art teacher came out of the meeting very upset, and I was allowed to go back to school.

CARLOS G.

He would rather bike three miles to town in ninety-degree weather to go to McDonald's than eat a quiet lunch at home with you. Why? Simple. Your grandson says, "Well, you see your friends there, and there's nobody to talk to around here."

● ● ● ● ●

The country grandsons are coming for a long weekend. Grandmother peers anxiously out of the window.

"Where can they be?" she asks.

Grandfather grunts. He is seated at a table with an album and a large stack of photographs in front of him.

"Oh, why are you doing that now? Most people stick their pictures in as soon as they're developed."

"I don't know any people like that. Besides, it will give the boys something to do."

"I was planning to take them to cultural events, experiences they don't have out there where they live."

"See how far you get with that."

"Well, how are we to entertain them? They're so rambunctious at twelve and ten."

"Let's take them to the movies."

"Four days in a row at the movies? We'd all be cross-eyed. Why did you have to ask them? I'm exhausted already."

"Look, if you're going to be walking on hot coals the entire time, I suggest we send them home by return mail."

The grandmother looked dejected.

"All right, then," Grandfather says, "I'll take care of the boys. They can give me a hand with these pictures. As I said, all boys enjoy sorting through old photos."

"Yes, well, you're a boy, too, and look how far *you* got."

• • • • •

"Grandpa, Grandma, come quickly. Look at this rash." The daughter-in-law sounds slightly hysterical. "He's had chickenpox and measles, what else is there to have?"

"Looks like the little fellow's fallen into the poison ivy," Grandpa says knowingly.

"Poison ivy in the city, in January?" The mother shakes her head unbelievingly.

"Do you really want me to tell you what I think it is?" Grandpa takes a deep breath.

"That's why I asked your advice."

"Well, I think it's a case of good old-fashioned fleas."

"Fleas!" The mother hurries her child out of the room. *(continued on next page)*

Wise Precaution
People who insist on eating with their fingers will be issued chopsticks.

"Caught off the dog, of course," Grandpa calls after her.

"Whatever made you tell her that?" Grandma asks. "Just as she was beginning to trust us."

"Don't fret. She said herself she wanted our opinion. And that must be a first."

• • • • •

Listening in. When there is total silence, they're cooking up something. If the silence is broken by high-pitched laughter, you can be sure they're telling dirty jokes. You are working unseen in the kitchen when the gang comes racing through shouting four-letter words. Suddenly they see you and stand, frozen, waiting to be reprimanded. Clear your throat. Say, "How bizarre, I didn't understand a word." And go on with the meal.

• • • • •

He's a big boy now, and when the grandmother caught him letting the cat bat the hamster, she gave him a cuff. Not so big a boy that he didn't run to his father, shouting, "Grandma walloped me."

The father is outraged. "Don't you ever lay a hand on my child."

"A good justified smack never hurt anyone, including you," Grandma retorts.

"We prefer the verbal approach."

"Oh, for heaven's sake, he was teasing the animals."

"Well, why didn't you say so?"

"You wouldn't have heard me. You were too busy being righteous."

"Maybe it was all right this time; just don't make a habit of hitting him."

Grandma asks herself how she could have produced so smug a child.

• • • • •

Why Stand Up?

"You let Mama rule you in everything, Grandpapa."

"Why, so I do," says Grandpapa.

"Then why don't you stand up like a man?" says Little Harry.

Grandfather looks queerly. "Because I like sitting down best, my dear," he said. "I am an old gentleman and standing fatigues me."

The Virginians
WILLIAM MAKEPEACE THACKERAY

A Celebration of Grandparents

Come to the party, grandparents all,
Flourish those batons, answer the call.
Unfurl your banners, turn up the lights,
Time to promote our grandparents' rights.

Come in your limos, come on your feet,
Spill out of buildings into the street,
Rise from your armchairs, up on your toes,
Prove to the world that anything goes.

We are a group whose voice must be heard,
Gather around and let's spread the word.
Tell that our cause is vital and good.
Come celebrate your grandparenthood.

How can you help but admire the ingenuity of a grandson whose voice has apparently broken prematurely? Queried, he confesses to lowering it deliberately so he doesn't have to sing in the school choir. He'll go far.

● ● ● ● ●

One afternoon your eleven-year-old grandchild arrives wearing a pair of chandelier earrings with large orange stones in the centers and the price still attached.

"Where did you get those?" you ask.

"I found them, in the five-and-ten," she says, looking out of the window.

Two matching earrings! "You *found* them in the five-and-ten?"

"They were just sitting there on the

(continued on next page)

counter and they looked so beautiful."

"Did you pay for them?"

"Oh, Grandma, you know I don't have that much money."

"And you know you don't take things you can't afford. So I'm afraid you'll have to return them to the store by yourself."

"Oh, Grandma, suppose I got caught."

"If you could remove them without being seen, I expect you can replace them the same way."

She begins to cry. "I promise I'll never do it again if you'll come with me."

So you relent, and off you go together.

"I found them in the 5 & 10."

She manages to replace the earrings, and because she's faced up to her light-fingeredness, you end up buying them for her.   • • • • •

It doesn't take much to make you realize that the grandchildren have moved into the electronic age, leaving you far behind.

You could always help your own children with their homework, except when the New Math arrived. But now, with the grandchildren, an even worse stumbling block has appeared: the computer.

They talk of floppy disks and kilobytes and you are forced to suggest they ask for their parents' help in translation. You feel particularly small when you overhear a grandchild asking your daughter,

"Do you think Granny's smart?"

"Of course she is. Why?"

"Because she doesn't even know what software is."

Well! you think. I'll learn, I'm not going to be left behind.

• • • • •

A not-so-young grandparent is understandably perturbed when the pre-teen granddaughter experiments with a high-risk activity such as skateboard riding on one hand.

You want to instill a note of caution without giving her the idea that she can never take a risk. To forbid serves no purpose; she'd most likely continue behind your back.

So! Had it occurred to you this behavior might be a cry for attention? Better discover right now the hidden reasons causing her to make this desperate statement. Better find out before she falls off that skateboard.   • • • • •

Dressing the Dream Grandparent

Grandparents would do well to abide by the following dress code:

No sweatshirts. No Nikes, Reeboks or sneakers.

For grandfathers: No gold chains, bracelets, ear and /or nose studs. No tee shirts with inspirational messages. No bomber jackets with fake fur collars. And never, ohmiGod never, a swinging shoulder bag.

Casual clothes are generally frowned on. To be on the safe side, wear button-down shirt collars, three-piece suits, summer or winter. This effectively separates the generations. And don't forget to carry an executive's hand-tooled leather briefcase, even if you are not an executive.

Grandmothers are not expected to wear eye-catching designs, and attention-getting colors are taboo. No plunging necklines, see-through blouses, or mini-skirts. In short, no "fun" clothes, very little makeup, and "controlled" hair. Suggested attire: tailored suits to match the grandfather's, worn with skirts, not slacks, and never, God forbid ever, Ray Bans.

The purpose of this code is to enable the grandparents to blend in with the other grandparents, and to divert attention from them so teenaged grandchildren can be spared the excruciating embarrassment of ever seeming even remotely connected.

Scene: A family dinner. The grandparents are trying to listen to their daughter, who has recently returned from a trip to Greece. But her account is interrupted and everyone's attention is taken by the grandson teasing his father about losing a set at tennis. Patience! Recognize that his self-assertion, however damaging to the flow of the general conversation, is still the most important thing going on. Besides, you can hear about Greece after he's gone to bed. (Try to explain this to your daughter.)

• • • • •

The apprehensive eleven-year-old granddaughter is rolling down the highway in the front seat beside her grandfather.

"What's the speed limit, Grandpa?"

"Yes, I know I'm going too fast, but I promised Grandma we wouldn't be late for dinner. Cheer up, we'll be there in an hour."

The granddaughter stares straight ahead. Then she tries again. "How long do you think it would take another driver to get where we are going?"

"Oh, in half the time," Grandpa says guiltily.

It's another story when your grandson is on the seat beside you. His repeated exhortations to "Floor it, Grandpa!" can turn you into a wreck at the wheel.

• • • • •

Just before the big football game on Saturday the following conversation took place.

Mother: "Grandma is coming to watch you play."

Child: "Must she?"

Mother: "But you love Grandma."

Child: "She might be wearing that red shirt she plays tennis in. That's something a kid would wear and she's not a kid."

When the conversation was repeated to the grandmother, she was mortified. However, she was determined not to miss the game.

"All right," she told her grandson. "I know how you feel about my clothes and when I get to the football field, I'll be suitably dressed and I won't recognize you. No, better still, I won't even get out of the car."

But she quickly forgot her good intentions and when her grandson scored a touchdown she honked her horn enthusiastically. After the game he came to the car in agony.

"How could you honk your horn? Everybody in school knows what it sounds like."

"How could everybody in school possibly know that?"

"Because when you come to pick me up you keep on tooting to let me know you're there."

In the future, the grandmother decided, she would keep away from the school until she had mastered this particular behavioral code.

• • • • •

Wise Precaution

Remember, it's an unimaginative child who raises his offspring exactly the way you raised yours.

BALLOONS

5. Thirteen to Seventeen:

WHEN SMILES TURN TO SCOWLS

A lot of scowls can be prevented by respecting the grandchild's privacy. For example, when a new friend, John, is brought over, don't ask what his last name is. That's really being intrusive. Besides, your grandson only knows him as John anyway. Should you have caused embarrassment, treat them at Burger King.

Grandfather had been a good amateur tennis player in his day. In fact, he once made the semifinals of the Regional Senior Men's Doubles Tournament. And now, wonder of wonders, a grandson was following in his footsteps. Grandfather took it upon himself to improve the boy's game. They'd meet at 7 a.m. on the courts, and after school there'd be calisthenics and more practice.

After a while Grandmother began to complain.

"Tennis, tennis, just you and he. Is this how you and I had planned to spend our free time?"

"He needs to keep at it," Grandfather explained. "I'm just giving him a few pointers. He's a natural, I tell you, there's nothing to prevent him grand-slamming it one day."

"You know, he might just want to be a good average player like you."

"When he has a chance to be a champ?"

"I think I'll ask him," said Grandmother. And she did.

It turned out that the boy, grateful for Grandfather's interest, didn't want to hurt his feelings, but he'd never thought of tennis as anything but a game to play with his friends, which he didn't have an opportunity to do anymore; and, frankly, he wasn't getting the workout he was used to.

Grandma relayed this conversation as tactfully as she could.

"Well, I think I'd better get back to my painting," Grandfather said, "since nobody wants to play tennis with me."

"I do," said Grandmother.

• • • • •

On first meeting a grandson's new girlfriend, don't try to maneuver him out of the room so you can interrogate her.

Helpful Hint
Try to avert your eyes from the acned part of the face. The child is more unhappy about it than you.

Teenager: Nobody else I know spends every evening with their grandmother.

Grandmother: Sorry about that, but if you want money to buy your day-glo makeup you'll have to allow your mother to go to work.

Teenager: Some kids have sitters, people more their own age.

Grandmother: Sitters cost money. No, I'm afraid until you're old enough to sit for yourself you're going to have to put up with me, and I might add that works both ways. Goodnight.

• • • • •

The granddaughter sits on a stool in the kitchen wearing a sleeveless blouse, a half slip, and an expression of martyrdom. The grandmother is peeling potatoes at the sink. When the mother returns from work, there are none of the usual exuberant greetings.

"Don't you have something to tell?" Granny prompts.

The girl hesitates.

"Shall I?" the grandmother says.

"No, I will." She pauses for effect. "While you were out, Mother, I became a woman."

• • • • •

Chilled to the bone after being caught in a downpour, the grandfather heads for home and a hot shower to find his granddaughter caroling in the bathroom. To make himself heard, he opens the door a crack.

"What are you doing in here, Grandpa? I'm bare."

"I can't see you through the curtain. Hurry up. I'm wet and cold."

"O.K.," she says, taking her time leaving.

Finally, the shivering grandfather gets into the shower and gets out again nicely warmed, and then:

"Damn it, you've taken my towel!"

Tossing the towel back into the bathroom, she says, "Please don't swear, Grandpa."

• • • • •

On a recent trip to California you bought a one-shouldered Latex swim suit for your thirteen-year-old granddaughter. She thanked you politely. Each day when she went swimming, however, she'd be wearing her old navy nylon with the high neckline. Finally you asked her why she never wore your present.

She didn't say a word, but the next morning she appeared in an oversized sweat shirt, the hem of your suit visible at the bottom.

How obtuse of you to forget that a budding figure must be carefully hidden from the outside world.

• • • • •

Princess Marie Louise was fifteen when she attended her first dinner party with her grandmother Queen Victoria at Balmoral. Marie Louise sat next to the Lord Chancellor and never spoke. Suddenly, the sepulchral voice of a footman murmured in her ear: "The Queen wishes the young princess to remember to entertain her neighbors at dinner."

Queen Victoria's Private Life
BY E. E. P. TISDALL

Grandparent: What's this long face all about?

Grandchild: Could be I'm adopted, could be some movie star gave me away...

Grandparent: Could be you're mad at your parents again.

• • • • •

The gang is inside. The friends have come over for the evening. Rock radio is on max. Everyone is eating and singing. There's not an empty chair. There's no place for you. Exit unnoticed. Go to the room after the next room and listen to the tunes. Get to know the groups. At least you'll have an idea what to give them for Christmas.

• • • • •

In a multigenerational house early morning rules must be strictly observed. The very youngest are awake as soon as it's light. They may get up and play with their toys provided they remain silent. Around eight, the next youngest are out of bed, full of pep. "Run outside," Grandpa tells them, "and don't bounce your ball against the house."

By now Grandpa is downstairs. He puts the coffee on, which wakes Grandma, and then the parents appear. Now we can all be as noisy as we like, and by noon even double the noise so that the teenagers are aroused in time for lunch.

• • • • •

House Rule
Noise is something you learn to live with again.

Page From the Diary of a 13-Year-Old

Dad says I shouldn't ask this, but I want to know anyway, how come you had this kid that's years younger than me, Grandpa? Why didn't you stay married to Grandma, then we wouldn't all be in this mess?

Dad says he also wishes you still were, too, but he says we must be friends and it will be all right.

But I don't think it will. I mean, I know you'll spend more time with the new kid, like you're living in the same house. We can't take a baby along on our camping trip, so what are you going to do? Stay here? I don't like it, Grandpa, it's a big trouble to me. Oh, why couldn't you just have stayed married to Grandma?

• • • • •

Teenager: Can I stay out until two?

Grandparent: Oh, you'd need to call your parents on that one (meaning you don't approve, you don't want the responsibility, and you don't want to have to be the one to say no).

• • • • •

Grandson: Did you say you and Grandma were going out tonight?

Grandpa: (immediately suspicious): And...

Grandson: Well, I'd like to ask some people over.

Grandpa: Why not tomorrow when we're home again?

Grandson: I'll clean up afterwards, I swear.

Grandpa: Like you did last year?

Grandson: I was only a kid then. Come on, Grandpa, say yes.

Grandpa: Well, no smoking and no drinking...

Grandson: Forget it, nobody'd come.

• • • • •

Wise Precaution
Be generous when advice is asked for and be pithy if you can.

"Grandpa, I Love You!"

The only thing I can tell you about being a grandparent is that it keeps me very busy on the phone. I have three grandchildren and keep changing my will every time one of them does something that pleases me. For example, two days ago my five-year-old grandson said to me, "Grandpa, I love you. Will you sit in the back of the car with me?" I immediately called my attorney and instructed him that the lad was to get EVERYTHING — even if it meant cutting off the other two.

Yesterday my youngest grandchild fell asleep in my lap. I decided right then and there he was entitled to a trust fund — even if it meant cutting off the other two.

This is the way it's been going for me for some time now. I haven't come to any resolution of the grandfather problem, but it's costing me a fortune in lawyer's fees.

ART BUCHWALD

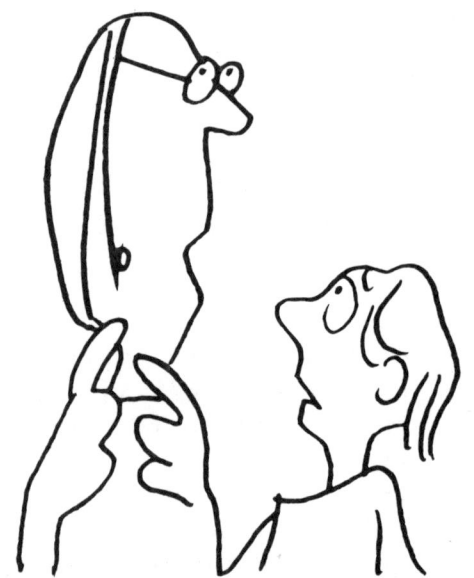

Granddaughter: If they're all smoking, what can I do? I don't want to seem like a wimp.

Grandparent: Don't say, "I'm not allowed to smoke." Say, "Thank you very much, I'm trying to quit."

• • • • •

Kitty litter time. Grandparent to grandson: How nice, I see you're going fishing. But, first, please change the kitty litter for me.

Grandson: Do I have to?

Grandparent: You know the rules. It's your turn.

Grandson (running off): I'll do it when I get back.

Oldest granddaughter comes in half awake.

Grandparent: When you've had breakfast, will you empty the cat box?

Granddaughter: I'm not eating breakfast. I was up very late last night. (Sees grandson leaving) Besides, it's his turn.

She runs after grandson.

As her son enters from the rear, she rushes to bar the front door.

Grandparent: Kitty litter time for you.

Son: For me? The children . . .

Grandparent: If you can't control your children, you'll have to do it yourself. It's your cat.

Son: I'll get the children.

• • • • •

When you ask your grandson to clean up his room and he responds with a temper tantrum, it is wise not to answer in kind. It's foolish to risk a physical confrontation with someone who's bigger than you and who's too old to be confined to quarters. Close the door instead. Tantrums are better worked out in private. And he might surprise you with a tidy room. He might.

• • • • •

Vacation on a Farm

Grandfather would take me down to the cowshed and let me milk the cows. "Be sure you get the last drops out," he'd say, "or that cow's going to be mighty uncomfortable."

"I know, I know," I'd tell him. But after the first steady stream of milk landed in the pail the cow would still be mighty uncomfortable. Then grandfather would put me aside and take over, twisting and pulling until he got the very last drop out.

"If a job's worth doing, it's worth doing well," he'd say, laughing, time and time again.

Sometimes I really hated grandfather.

CHARLOTTE PETHERICK

Places to be Photographed in New York

And Suggested Appropriate Poses
(Grandson Version)

When he was a small boy visiting New York, the grandson sent his friends photos of himself standing in the shadow of the Statue of Liberty.

Now the mood has changed. Here in random order is a list of where to be seen and how:

1. Washington Square: doing kick-outs and inverts and slides on your skateboard.
2. Bronx Zoo: gripping the cage bars and imitating a monkey.
3. Times Square video arcade: feeding the machines, wearing a painter's hat on the back of your head.
4. Central Park South and Fifth Avenue: Your face next to a lifesize cardboard reproduction of Ronald Reagan.
5. Tower Records: laden with shopping bags of tapes and records.
6. Crazy Eddie's: laden with more shopping bags.
7. Port Authority Bus Terminal: looking like a runaway. (A real coup would be to get a cop to pose with you gripping your arm.)
8. Subway platform: holding a tin cup.
9. Famous Night Spot: displaying the name prominently in the picture, wearing Bermuda shorts with underwear showing.

And lastly, for old times' sake, why not? Your picture in the shadow of the Statue of Liberty. To show you really made it to the Big Apple.

"Here's your grandson with a spiked Mohawk.

"What do you think, Gran?" he asks knowingly.

Don't gasp. "Well, it's different, dear."

He sees right through you. "No sweat, it's not a radical and it's not dyed."

"But the roots are showing," you can't help saying.

"That's all part of it, Gran, roots should show."

Just hope he'll soon meet some nice girl who'll have her own ideas about hair styles.

• • • • •

Grandfather and his son are having a game of chess, sitting together in companionable silence, and then in comes the grandson, home from school.

Son (with rather heavy joviality): Welcome home! How was hockey practice?

Grandson: Okay.

Son: Are you breaking in those new skates we bought?

Grandson: Why are you always cross-examining me?

He stalks out noisily.

Son: What shall I do?

Grandfather: Ignore him. He's only trying to grow up.

Son: Damn teenagers... And it was so sudden. A couple of months ago, he followed me around everywhere.

Grandfather: He'll come back. You did.

Son: Listen, I never behaved like that.

Grandfather (laughs): Oh, a memory block, I see.

• • • • •

Never attempt their language.

Grandpa (with fishing rod): Hey, man, wanna ride with the tide?

Grandson: What?

Grandpa: I thought that's the way you talk.

Grandson: We used to.

• • • • •

Mother: Who took that last piece of melon from the refrigerator?

Grandson: Well, I did...

Mother: Didn't you know I'd been saving it for my breakfast?

Grandmother: And didn't you know I'd been saving it for tonight's dessert?

• • • • •

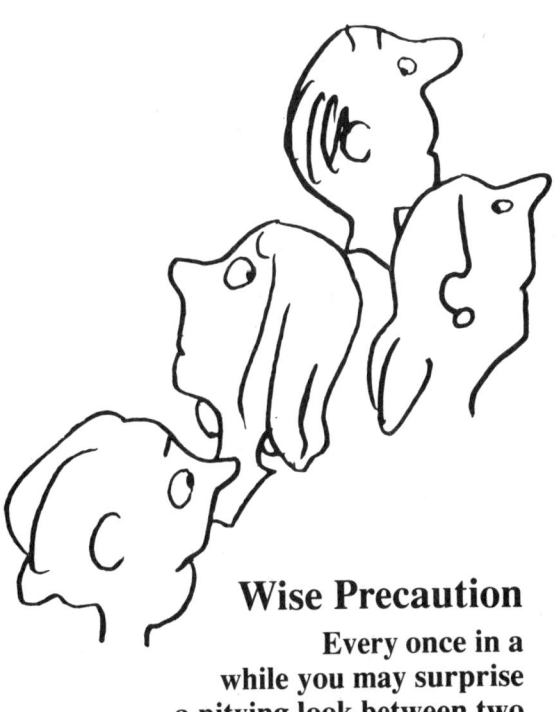

Wise Precaution

Every once in a while you may surprise a pitying look between two grandchildren. Pretend you didn't see.

"Oh," she says to her mother, "I'd rather go shopping with Grandma than you, any day."

"Sure," says the mother, "because you think she'll let you buy anything you want. But I know Grandma will be sensible this time."

So off they go, grandmother and granddaughter, and after a full afternoon of visiting shops, she spies a fringed mini skirt with a cosmic design embroidered in sequins. "Oh, I'd really like that," she says. "Please, Grandma, please!"

Well, she certainly picked a dilly, Grandma thinks to herself, but if it means so much to her, I'll risk it.

The mother greets them at the door, shakes her head.

"That's absolutely the last time you two go shopping together," she says.

• • • • •

Parental rules seem to differ for each child; grandparents should keep their ears open.

"No," you say, left alone with your daughter's child, "definitely not. You cannot take the TV apart."

"I've fixed it before."

"No, I said."

"All right, I'll stop. It's just like Mother told me." She shakes her head and looks resigned.

"Just what did Mother tell you?"

"I can't remember."

"Go on."

"Well," she said, "'Grandma's of another generation and she sometimes understands completely differently and if you don't get it, just do what she says,' and that's what's happening now."

• • • • •

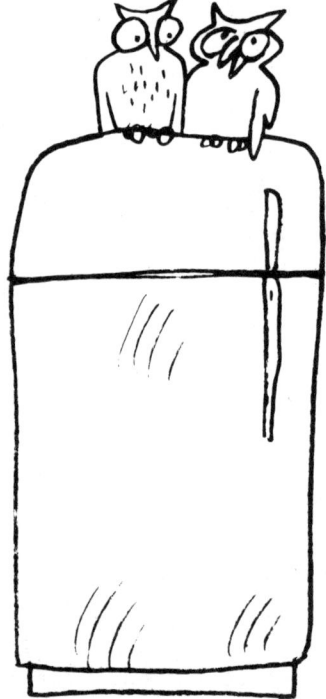

Wise Precaution

Living alone the two of you have forgotten the size of teenagers' appetites and since they often drop in unannounced, it makes sense to keep your refrigerator well stocked with their favorite foods. Otherwise you could find yourselves without the essentials for the next meal.

> Nor thy tailor, rascal, who is thy grandfather: he made these clothes, which as it seems make thee.
>
> *Cymbeline,* ACT IV, SC. 2

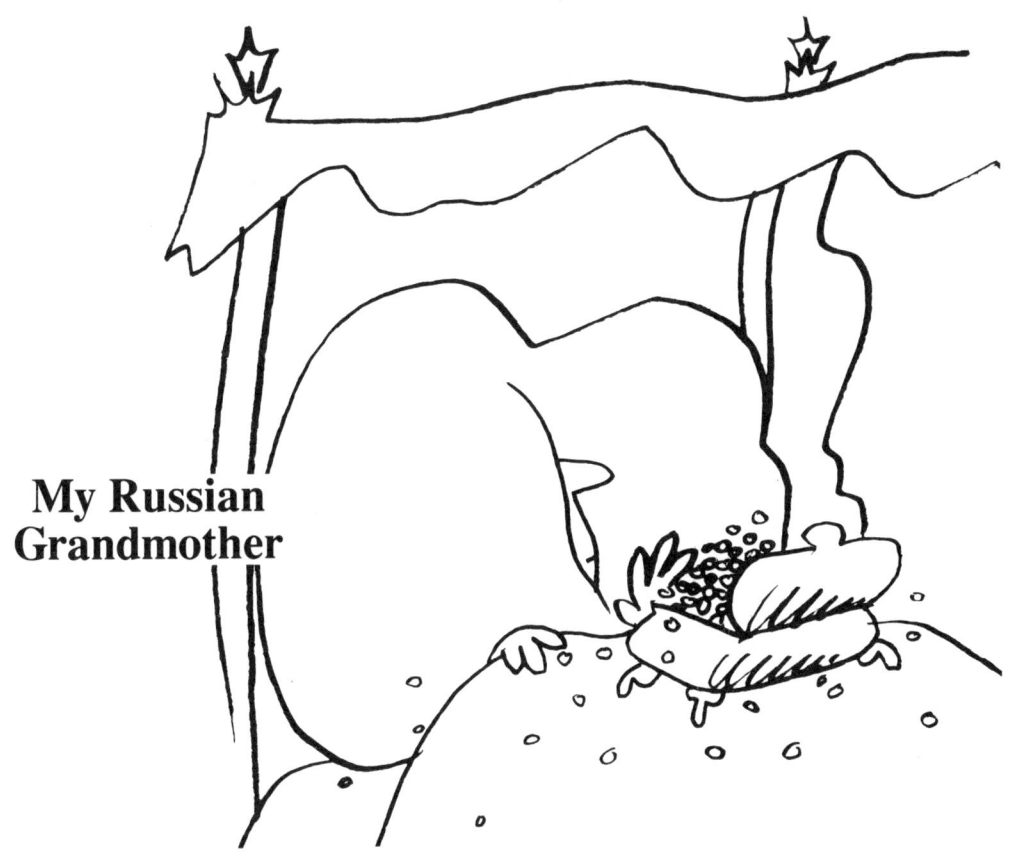

My Russian Grandmother

My maternal grandmother was the sole heiress of a large estate. When she was a child there were still serfs, whose children, younger than herself, were the dolls she played with. Oh, I understand your reaction, but that's how it was in the late 19th century.

As a young woman she was beautiful, intellectual, and dressed by Worth. Then she married my grandfather, who was interested in preserving the estate. They went to live there, where she was isolated and unhappy.

My grandmother slept in a cork-lined room to help her insomnia, and hypnotists came to cure her. She took many pills. In fact, fleeing the revolution for France, her suitcases were filled with pills. No jewels, just pills.

In France every Sunday after Mass I was obliged to visit her. My grandmother would take my face under the chin, turn it to one side and say, "You look like your papa," turn it around and say, "This side is like mama." By this time, in Paris, she had resumed all her intellectual pursuits and was happy again.

SOPHIE WINKELHORN

Bonding of women. When your granddaughter is visiting and goes out on dates, you leave your bedroom door open so that you can hear when she is safely home. Too, she might want to recap a lovely evening, but tonight you hear the sounds of muffled sobbing as she passes your door. Should you interfere? You do.

"Come in and tell me all about it," you say. She does, after some comforting.

"Johnny brought me home with Muffie, who was going to spend the night. But then she and Johnny went off to another party and didn't ask me. And, oh, Grandma, he was my date."

"That's the way some dates are," you tell her. "He's certainly not worth crying over. Isn't that so, Grandpa?"

But Grandpa feigns sleep.

Helpful Hint

Eye control used to be a good weapon when confronting a small child in an out-and-out lie. However, it's futile to try and outstare a teenager, because his eyes are usually fixed on the floor anyway.

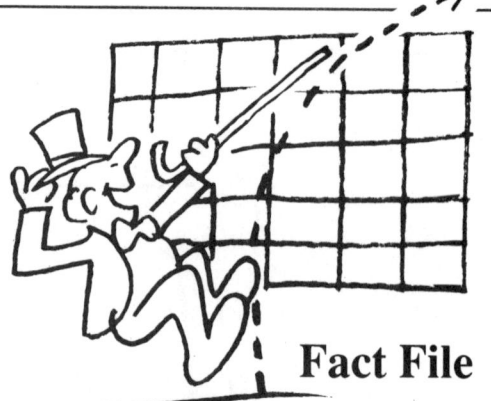

Fact File

Twenty-six million Americans are over 65. Eighty percent of them have had at least one child; that's 20 million, and 95 percent of them have had a grandchild. So that makes 19 million grandparents.

• • • • •

Sunday lunch. Grandpa, at the carving board: Who's ready for a second helping?

Son-in-law: Sorry, we have to be at the first tee in a few minutes.

Grandpa to grandson: Well, how about you?

Grandson (making faces to his friends outside the window): Everything.

Grandpa: Tell your friends to go away until we've finished eating.

Grandson: Thanks, but I won't have any more, after all.

Grandpa: Well, then, you'd better all go.

Daughter: And don't you do a thing about the dishes.

(They all exit.)

Grandma: As a matter of fact, I don't think we will.

Grandpa: What would you say to switching Sunday lunch to Sunday dinner?

Grandma: Or forgetting the whole thing.

BALLOONS

6. Eighteen Up:

ADDING UP THE SCORE

And now they are starting to test their wings. They are beginning to say goodbye. Be prepared to welcome them back. And, when they do come, one hopes, you will have a grandchild you can treat as an equal. It's your fault if you don't also have a friend.

Grandfather: I simply can't get over the change in the boy. You can actually have a sensible conversation without getting your head bitten off. Who would have guessed?

Grandmother: It's always a bit chancy but most of them seem to turn out all right in the end.

Grandfather: In fact he mentioned he might like to go to my alma mater — something his father never considered. I said I'd pull a few strings if he really buckled down.

Grandmother: Go ahead and pull strings before he makes another choice.

Grandfather: Let me get to that phone!

• • • • •

He's a late-blooming seventeen, and you can tell this worries him. He stands listlessly watching his grandfather lug in the firewood.

Grandfather: Why are you moping around?

Grandson: I've got nothing to do.

Grandfather: You can help me carry these logs.

Grandson: I meant nothing interesting to do. It's such a drag. Boring.

Grandfather: At your age I'd spend hours thinking about who I was, and that can be very boring, but then I met a girl and began to think of her. Be patient. It will happen to you.

Grandson: It will? *(continued on next page)*

Grandfather (nodding): Of course, it might come quicker if you started interesting yourself in other people's concerns now. (He laughs and looks down at his armful of wood.)

Grandson (laughing, too): Something like, "Here, let me give you a hand with those logs?"

Grandfather: Something like that.

Clothes and looks are a statement not to be taken lightly.

Avoid criticizing the way they dress. How would you like it if you were all dressed up and someone said you looked awful?

Clothes and looks are a statement that should not be taken lightly, even when it's a safety pin piercing the ear or neon-colored hair. One grandchild, when asked why he sported an eye-catching wardrobe, said, "So I won't be invisible."

Choosing their own clothes makes them conscious of taste and is a small but important step towards independence. A truthful grandparent would admit that the real objection to a carefully considered costume in purple and saffron is the terrible fear that a friend might mistake your grandchild's taste for your own.

The grandparents are getting dressed for a dinner party.

Grandpa: That grandson will drive me nuts, always borrowing...

Grandma: Money?

Grandpa: No, clothes.

Grandma: Thank God.

Grandpa: I searched everywhere for this tuxedo vest, and where did I find it? Behind a chair in his room, and covered with beer stains, no less. How can I wear something like this?

Grandma: I'm not saying I approve of borrowing, dear. But I think he must be expressing something...

Grandpa: I wish he'd express it by taking his father's things.

• • • • •

Just because your knowledge of drugs is nil, do not be caught thinking "Impossible. I've always had a quiescent grandchild." It's up to you to know if Mt. Etna is waiting to erupt just below that tranquil surface.

Be aware of such signs as: when their moods change; when they wander home in the middle of the night; when they tell fanciful stories; when they seem to have a constant cold; when tempers are at a breaking point; when they hide in their rooms and avoid their old friends.

By now, you have only yourself to blame if you're not thinking drugs.

• • • • •

Home Rule
No shoes, coats, or sporting equipment may be dropped just inside the front door.

Not many people can boast of having had three grandparents in Congress. Can you guess who they are?

Answer: The children of former Senator Howard H. Baker, Jr. Both Howard H. Baker, Sr. and his wife served in the House of Representatives. Mrs. Howard H. Baker, Jr. was the daughter of the late Senator Everett M. Dirksen of Illinois.

All afternoon Grandma has been calling the house to see if her grandson is home for dinner. All she gets is a busy signal. Forget it, she tells herself.

Once home, as expected, she finds her grandson sprawled in a chair, talking animatedly into the telephone. He acknowledges her with a small wave.

As Grandma puts away the groceries, her grandson saunters into the kitchen.

"What's for dinner, Grandma?"

(continued on next page)

Great Grandad

Twenty-one boys and not one bad.
They never got fresh with old grandad.
If they had he'd have been quite glad
To tan their hides with a hickory gad.

They grew strong in heart and hand,
Firm foundation of our land,
Twenty-one boys and a great grandson.
He has a terrible time with that one.

OZARK FOLK SONG

(continued from page 87)

"Sorry," she says, "I couldn't get through to you this afternoon, so I didn't buy you anything. Take a look in the refrigerator and see what you can find for yourself. Incidentally, that must have been a very important conversation to take so long. Who were you talking to?"

"Oh, just working the phones."

• • • • •

These cries come from those waiting to hear about college acceptance. The grandparents' reassurance is sought, because of their past experience.

Nervous: I thought I'd done all right, but now I'm not so sure.

Guilty: You'll tell Dad how hard I've been studying, won't you, Grandpa? He'll listen to you.

Doubtful: Why did they insist on a big school instead of some Joe Cool College that I could easily make?

Anticipatory: I told them to mail the reply to you and Grandpa so my mother can't steam it open first.

Puzzled: Maybe my marks haven't been sensational, I told my parents, to let them down easy. I also told them I might not be college material. But that doesn't mean I'm stupid, does it, Grandma?

Impatient: It's the waiting I can't take, makes me want a six-pack.

My Grandfather, Avon Long

I remember how I used to walk down the long, dark hallway, making sure not to bump into anything. Finally, I would reach my destination. I'd push open the door slowly, to be greeted by huge clouds of smoke; there was always a cigarette burning. Looking beyond the ashtray, I'd see the proof of long, hard nocturnal attempts to fall asleep as there were many faded, worn-out crossword puzzles, books, a huge dictionary, and pairs of reading glasses.

Finally, with eyes fixed on the blurry TV screen, there lay my grandfather, in a huge bed. He'd turn around and catch a glimpse of me standing there, smiling, and all at once his eyes would squint with glee, his mouth would open wide, and he'd yell out my name, "Stephanie!"

My grandfather was a very special man. He was a performer on Broadway and at the Cotton Club. He was well known for his club acts and movie roles. He always had  something deep and profound to say. He sure knew how to liven up a place... yelling here, laughing there.

I am glad to share his story with you because it's almost as if he were there again, in that bed, yelling my name out or watching TV.

Grandpa, I miss you!

STEPHANIE MARSHALL

Desperate: Who'd take me? I might as well kill myself now, get it all over with.

That's the cry that makes the grandparents come running.

• • • • •

The conversation takes place before the arrival from college of the grandson and his girlfriend for the weekend.

"Give me a hand, will you," says the grandmother, flicking a sheet over the bed at the grandfather. *(continued on next page)*

"Why don't we make up the double bed, give them more room?"

"They are not sharing any double bed."

"It's not like this will be the first time."

"In my house it will."

She tugs the sheet taut on her side, leaving him with too little to tuck in.

He looks at her. "I never thought you were prudish."

"I feel a responsibility to her mother."

"I don't see why I should be considered square just because you are."

He tosses a pillow on her side of the bed.

"So that's what's bothering you." She laughs. "Go ahead and tell them that you would be perfectly happy to let them share a room. Blame it all on me. I have a broad back."

"Oh, shut up."

"This is my laundry!"

The granddaughter arrives from college with a full backpack and four bursting shopping bags. "So much luggage, what a pleasure!" you say. "I thought you could spend only one night."

"Right," she answers, putting down the backpack and four bags, "this is my laundry."

Always check the grandchildren's room before they leave to avoid having to express-mail forgotten tennis racquets, ski boots, and similar heavy objects, which the owner now needs immediately.

• • • • •

You come into the living room and find your granddaughter and her boyfriend entwined on the sofa. At your entrance, they spring apart, and he flees without speaking.

"Dear," you say to your granddaughter, "I don't think you and your friend should cuddle up like that. When I was young . . ."

"But when you were young, Grandma, you were never left alone with your boyfriend. And Grandma, you don't really know what temptation is, do you?"

• • • • •

Every young woman is permitted to make one or two mistakes in the choice of a boyfriend. And this granddaughter used up one of these mistakes when she invited her latest to visit.

Some of the discards had been more attractive than others, some less, but this one is dreadful.

Big of head and massive of thigh, he fills the room with insecurity. So you escape to your corner and relax over a game of solitaire, leaving your granddaughter to entertain her guest. He follows you to the table, full of bonhomie.

"Playing solitaire, Grandma?" he asks. (Grandma!) "Well, you know the real game is to use two decks. Bring me another," he orders your granddaughter, then sweeps up your unfinished game and demonstrates. *(continued on next page)*

When I lean like this
I can make out old Grandsir Stark
  distinctly —
With his pipe in his mouth and his
  brown jug —
Bless you, it isn't Grandsir Stark,
  it's Granny.
But the pipe's there and smoking and
  the jug.
She's after cider, the old girl, she's
  thirsty.
Here's hoping she gets her drink . . .

"Generations of Men"
ROBERT FROST

Or you are making a sauce for the baked chicken when this one interrupts again. He sticks a finger in the saucepan, licks it, and says,

"Good, but it could use a dash of crystallized ginger."

This is actually not such a bad idea, but you'll be damned if you take it.

Your granddaughter follows you around for an opportunity to be alone, which you are anticipating and avoiding.

"How do you like him, Grandma?" she says eventually, cornering you. "Isn't he the best?"

What good will it do to tell her what you really think? In the face of true love any criticism is bound to be resented. So you simply say:

"He seems extremely capable, dear." And hope he will disappear as suddenly as he arrived.

● ● ● ● ●

Granma and Granpa raced each other to get across the yard. They fought over everything and loved and needed the fighting.

The Grapes of Wrath
JOHN STEINBECK

It is the day after the grandson's graduation, the mood is mellow, and Grandpa is ready for a serious, man-to-man talk.

Grandpa: Good show, Skipper, and now it's the real world. Any idea what you'll be doing out there? (The grandson shrugs.) It's not so easy to get a job.

Grandson: You see ads for sales clerks and supermarket baggers every way you turn.

Grandpa (Rolling his eyes to the ceiling): Is this why I sent him to college? Don't you have any ... grander plans?

Grandson: I wouldn't mind seeing what it's like to be a plumber ...

Grandpa: Plumbers certainly make good money, if that's what you're looking for. But, plumbers have very long hours. How about joining the family firm?

Grandson: Oh, plumbers, carpenters, painters, you know what I mean, I thought I might try to see what the inside of a house is all about. If it doesn't work out, I'll find something else.

Grandpa: Saves time if you decide what you want to be early. Houses, you say? Could we have a budding architect on our hands right here?

Grandson: Oh, lay off, Grandpa, you didn't hear a word I said.

Helpful Hint
If you give an order and the grandchild asks, "Why?", explain. They deserve something better than "Because I say so, that's why."

My Chinese Grandmother

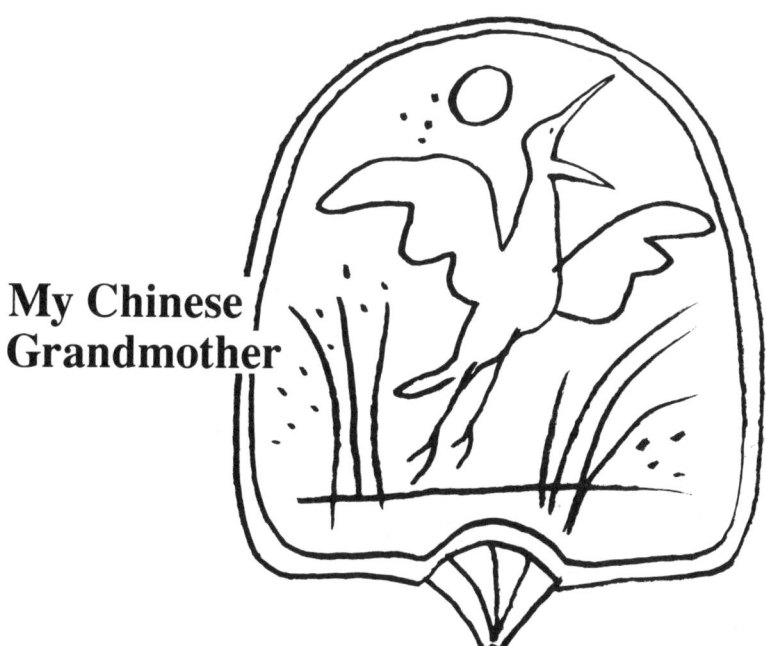

My Chinese grandmother was widowed early. If you are widowed in China, customs dictate, you never remarry, and my grandmother never did. She just continued on. In China, we were one big family that lived together under the same roof. My father came to the United States by himself around 1950. The family joined him about six years later. My grandmother, however, stayed in China.

The next time I saw her was more than a quarter of a century later when I went back to Hong Kong for a visit. I should say that was the first time I really saw her because I was too small in China to have any firm recollection or impression of her. She was frail but the lines on her face and the steely fierceness in her eyes showed a toughness inside born of long years of loneliness endured in silence. I was told one of her delights, if there were any, was to drink brandy out of rice bowls.

A few years later my father brought her to New York. Here, everyone has his own job, the hours are different, the life very independent. We were very seldom together under one roof. She must have felt a great disappointment. After spending so many years by herself in China, she now spent the days by herself in New York. There was no more dream to sustain her. She died two years later of natural causes, but we found a knife under her pillow.

ROBIN C. C. WU

Keep in the background during the preparations for your granddaughter's wedding. At the reception, control your urge to dance. Seat yourself at an inconspicuous table with the other grandparents, and forget that you have footed most of the bills.

• • • • •

After the wedding, when everything has settled back to normal, the grandparents began thinking about their future and decided they might like to spend their winters in a warmer climate.

"Just to see if we like it," they told their children.

"Won't be in one of those retirement homes where the average age is seventy," said the Grandfather.

"Why, that should make you feel quite at home," Grandmother laughed.

"Age hasn't softened you, has it?" he retorted. And they both had to agree he'd won that round.

So they spent a pleasant summer looking over brochures. Just after Christmas they started the cross-country drive, three hours for him, two for her, until they reached New Mexico.

It was a happy choice, and they were enjoying themselves to the hilt when they received a call from their eldest daughter.

"You must come home."

They pressed around the telephone, each holding onto the receiver.

"Tell us, what's happened?"

The answer, when it came, was not unexpected.

"You're going to be great-grandparents," she said.

• • • • •

Home Rule

Respect their political rules, however different they are from your own. If the grandchildren are allowed to express themselves freely, you may find disagreements between you diminishing.

BALLOONS

Published by Spectacle Lane Press